Revolution Now ac[illegible] infecting society. In all human relationships a revolutionary change is necessary. But to be permanent and effective in solving man's problems, it must start at the root source of the infection.

Tying luscious golden fruit on the rotten branches of the old tree may satisfy today's appetite, but it will not solve tomorrow's hunger problem. The real problem is personal, individual, and that is where the therapy must begin.

In the following pages you will discover why revolution is needed, what form it should take, what it will accomplish and how it can be produced. YOU can get involved in the "Revolution Now," for it is essentially a personal experience.

REVOLUTION NOW!

Bill Bright

Campus Crusade for Christ, Inc.
Arrowhead Springs, San Bernardino, California 92404

REVOLUTION NOW
By Bill Bright

Simultaneously published in Canada.
Printed in the United States of America.

First Printing, July, 1969
Second Printing, September, 1969
Third Printing, November, 1969
Fourth Printing, February, 1970
Fifth Printing, June, 1970
Sixth Printing, December, 1970

To My Father and Mother

whose love and prayers are a constant source of spiritual strength and encouragement; and between whom and their children there has never been a generation gap.

Foreword

We live in the most revolutionary period of human history. Campus disorders have assumed epidemic proportions! Not only turbulent Berkeley, but also staid Harvard, has staggered under the blows and strikes of the dissidents and militants. Civil authorities pray for cool summers to quiet the nerves of the inner cities. Urban problems continue to increase in number and gravity.

Leaders of the "Establishment" work around the clock in their attempt to find band-aids large enough for the festering wounds. At the same time, leaders of the militant groups are formulating procedures for major surgery.

What does the future hold? Is there hope for a solution? Can a vaccine be discovered in time to save our world's sick society? For almost 20 years it has been my privilege to speak to tens of thousands of students and professors from hundreds of campuses around the world. The rich rewards of these experiences have convinced me that there is a solution.

About 2,000 years ago—through the birth of the greatest Revolutionary in history—a vaccine became available that will destroy the moral virus infecting today's society. Social band-aids and reform antiseptics give little hope for a cure or even an improvement. A revolution is needed.

I have seen men and women from all walks of life commit themselves to this Revolutionary. The result? A complete transformation, resulting in true freedom, happiness and purpose.

This greatest Revolutionary gives release from the guilt and frustrations of the past. He offers a challenge and a cause worth living for. He provides the only hope for the mortal ills of our society.

The world needs a revolution—the right kind of a revolution. One that will build, not destroy. One that will propagate love, not hatred. A revolution that will bring equality, not suppression. One that will restore man to God's image, rather than debase him to a bestial level.

You can experience this revolution. In fact, you can help bring it to pass.

I invite you to meet the greatest Revolutionary of all the centuries. You will never be the same. And the world will be further changed if you join the REVOLUTION NOW.

Bill Bright

Arrowhead Springs 1969

Contents

Chapter 1

A Call to Revolution

In this desperately critical and chaotic hour when the entire world is engulfed with a spirit of revolution, millions of men and women are looking for a leader to follow and a cause to which they can give themselves with total commitment. Dr. Nathan Pusey, president of Harvard University, said, "The youth of this generation are looking for a flag to wave, a creed to believe and a song to sing."

It is the hour of opportunity for those who are seeking to bring peace and fulfillment to our fragmented and frustrated world. But an opportunity is only an opportunity, a chance is only a chance. What counts is what one is able to make of it. Nicholas Murray Butler, former president of Columbia University, said, "I divide the world into three classes—the few who make things happen; the many who watch things happen; and the overwhelming majority who have no notion of what happens."

Never have there been so many people knowing so much, having so much and experiencing so much. The horizons are wider, the potentials are greater and the tempo is faster than ever before.

And tomorrow promises to be even more exciting! Human knowledge and technology have shifted into overdrive. Unless a Ph.D. continues to study, he is obsolete in three years. We are told that knowledge doubles every five years. Ninety percent of all scientists who have ever lived are living today. Space technicians no longer speak of moon orbits, but of moon colonies. In medical circles there are persistent rumors of brain transplants. With incredible rapidity mini-computers are crowding out human brawn and brain.

The Other Side

But there is another side of this coin. It is dirty and bloody and stinks of arson and reefers. This is a day of crime, urban violence, racial strife and destructive demonstrations. This Hydra-headed monster bares its deadly fangs in universities and communities around the world. In recent elections both major parties have promised to give urban crime and unrest top priority rating on their list of reforms.

In our great cities many churches have discontinued all evening services. It is no longer safe for good people to go to church. Police teams patrol the corridors of public schools. The silent majorities in our great universities are muzzled by fear of knives and clubs. The new morality has made chastity a rare exception. The world of entertainment glorifies perversion and makes promiscuous sex the trademark of American culture.

"Winless" wars and prevaricating governments of the world reap their harvests of defiance and frustration.

Underneath all these frightening characteristics of our day, the diabolical manipulations of international communism are bringing us ever closer to universal tryanny. According to present schedules, and apart from a spiritual revolution through divine intervention, communist conquest of the world is assured in this generation.

Ours is a world in trouble! Dr. Pitirim Sorokin, noted Harvard sociologist, said, "Not only war, famine, pestilence, and revolution, but a legion of other calamities are rampant all over the entire world. All values are unsettled; all norms are broken. Mental, moral, aesthetic and social anarchy reigns." He was right and the evidence is increasingly clear. The facts are before us as we look about us and hear the reports.

Newspaper headlines tell the story. One issue of *The Daily Californian*, newspaper of the University of California, Berkeley, California, carried these headlines, "1,000 Students Stage March Around Campus," "Incidents Disrupt Classes," and "TWLF Continues Strike, Demands Radical Change." Scores of college campuses are in a state of chaos as riots and demonstrations threaten to destroy our educational system. Anarchy reigns. In one year both the president of the Southern Christian Leadership Conference, Dr. Martin Luther King, and Senator Robert Kennedy, leading contender for Democratic nomination for President of the United States, were assassinated.

A New Low

Multitudes of people have no share in any element

of greatness. Man has become a lowly creature of discouragement and defeat. There are racial discord, corruption in government, dishonesty in business and labor, and moral problems. Right now there are five million alcoholics in the United States. Every year the number increases by 50,000. Over half the hospital beds in our nation are filled with the mentally ill. There are over four million unwanted children. One out of five abortions ends in death. Suicide is the number two killer of teenagers. These are all symptoms of a sick society.

There is a crisis on the college campus. Not long ago I had opportunity to talk with a counselor at one of the dormitories at the University of California at Berkeley. As we talked about student problems he told me of how only a day before parents had come to pick up their 17-year-old son and take him to a mental hospital. He had been an Eagle Scout. He was sharp, clean-cut, and had a good high school record. The future for him was bright. Yet, when he got to Berkeley, something happened. He was given an IBM number. He did not meet anyone except the prostitutes on Telegraph Avenue and the dope pushers. Soon it was all over. He was hooked. The campus machine had failed. It could not give him the personal relationships which make life meaningful. He represents thousands of lost students among the seven million who are studying on the campuses of our land.

Another student chose to end his life rather than face the anguish of the future. Before committing suicide he left this note, "To anyone in the world who cares: Who am I? Why am I living? Where am I going? Life has become stupid and purposeless. Nothing makes sense any more. The questions I had when I came to college are still unanswered and now I am convinced that there are no answers. There can only be pain and guilt and despair here in this world. My fear of death and the unknown is far less terrifying than the prospect of the unbearable frustration, futility, and hopelessness of continued existence."

Revolution in Science

Revolution has occurred in nearly every area of life. In communications, for example, in 1950 there were 18 million auto radios and 81 million home radios. Today there are 64 million auto radios and 188 million home sets. The total, 252 million, represents more than one for every American. During the same time the number of black and white television sets has gone from 10 million to 88 million. There are now 10 million color sets in use. In 1950, there were none.

Transportation has shown an even more radical growth. It took 1,900 years to go from horse and burro power to the internal combustion engine. Approximately fifty years passed between its application to the airplane and the automobile to the advent of jet power. Now we have reached the moon through rocket power. It is amazing that the first atomic-powered submarine was launched in 1954, the first Sputnik in 1957, and the first man in space in 1961, that most college students today have never flown on anything but jets. Yet, by and large, man is not happier. Some picture the city dweller as a robot swaying on the subway as he goes to work. If he is in New York, he is one of the two million going in and out of the city every day—more than the entire population of Philadelphia—victimized rather than benefited by technology.

Political Revolution

Politically, the world is a vastly different place than it was twenty years ago. In that short time 43 countries have been admitted to the United Nations. Colonialism has all but disappeared, and the world has divided itself into three major blocks: the West, the Communists, and the Third World. All are vying for their own rights. One marvels that we hold together as a civilization. And that is precisely the point.

The revolutions have produced vast pockets of discontent. The college student rebels at being assigned a number. Communications have in many cases made people more aware of problems than of solutions. The technological advance has often widened the gap between groups of people rather than narrowed it. Man has become lost in his own achievements. H. L. Mencken expressed it this way: "The cosmos is a gigantic flywheel making 10,000 revolutions a minute. Man is a sick fly taking a dizzy ride on it. The basic fact about human experience is not that it is a tragedy, but that it is a bore. It is not that it is predominately painful, but that it is lacking in any sense."

Futile Attempts

Recognizing the danger of universal chaos, many sincere leaders in government and social service are attempting to extinguish the fire through poverty programs and improved industrial conditions. University administrators are seeking to personalize the college campus. Yet they often fall short. Clearly a breakthrough is needed.

The director of the Urban League recently wrote of his attempts to deal with some of the black man's problems, "The real estate man or the builder says the problem is economics; business or the employer says the problem is education; and the educators say the problem is a matter of housing . . . I go to the employer and ask him to employ Negroes, and he says, 'It's a matter of education.' Then I go to the educators and they say, 'If Negro people lived in good neighborhoods and had more intelligent dialogue in their families, more encyclopedias in their homes, more opportunity to travel, and a stronger family life, then we could do a better job of educating them.' And when I go to the builder he says, 'If they had the money, I would sell them the houses.' I am back at the employer's door again, where I started to begin with."

Who has solutions? What can be done? Some see no hope, as Bertrand Russell, who writes of basing one's life on a "firm foundation of unshakable despair." But most of us cannot take that way out—we want to take action—to make things happen. In spite of the fact that many of our generation have been described as more interested in security than in growth, in existence than in greatness, most of us can be moved to do something when someone brings us a plan that promises solutions. Change is something we must have!

Politicians and sociologists either admit their impotency or propagate meaningless and impractical theories and quack cures. Let's face it—our only hope is REVOLUTION. Young people know this and demonstrate for it. Unfortunately, they do not always know what they mean by "revolution."

"I am a revolutionist. I don't like this world and I want to help change it," snapped a zealous young campus radical, his eyes flashing with fire and hatred. "This older generation has made a mess of this world, and my generation is going to do something about it," he continued.

"I agree with you," I said. "The world is in a desperate plight and we must do something about the problems that face mankind now; but first, let us define the issues and then proceed to some logical conclusions and possible solutions."

We discussed the basic problems of racial inequality, social injustice, illiteracy, poverty, war and a few of lesser concern. As we talked, my student friend, who had never traveled extensively in other countries, was a bit surprised to learn that discrimination against minority races and groups is not limited to the United States. In Japan, the Koreans are subject to discrimination; in India, the caste system still prevails. In certain African countries, no white person is allowed citizenship. Every country has its privileged and its deprived.

Man is basically so self-centered and self-seeking that if all our problems should suddenly be solved, we would soon manufacture more. Senator George Aiken of Vermont observed, "If we were to wake up some morning and find that everyone was the same race, creed and color, we would find some other causes for prejudice by noon." Further, a brief review of history reminds us that the two most literate countries in the world, Germany and Japan, were responsible for World War II. So, obviously, illiteracy is not our biggest problem, nor will mass education provide the magic wand.

"You say that you are a revolutionary and you want to help change the world? So do I. I am unwilling to accept status quo. The problems which concern you, concern me and most other Christians as well." Our radical friend was surprised. But why should he be?

Revolution by Force and Fear

There are two major ways to change status quo; one is good and the other is bad. There is the revolution of force and fear which pits man against man, nation against nation, race against race. And there is the revolution of love and reason, a spiritual revolution which includes both God and man. I subscribe to the latter because history has confirmed that this is the only lasting way to promote a revolution that will accomplish the most good for all men of all races in all nations.

The way of force and fear has been tried and found wanting through the centuries. A madman can destroy in minutes what other men of brilliance and dedication have created and built over a period of generations. Raymond Moley, well-known writer and student of political history, said: "Real revolutions, unlike the American revolution, involve political, economic, and social change. They pass through three main phases. The first, if successful, destroys the traditional power structure and causes the death or exile of the people in control. In the second phase, the revolutionary forces turn on themselves in the struggle for power. The itch for power is disguised by charges of counterrevolution, or, in communist terms, 'deviation.' Finally, in the chaos or the uneasy hegemony that emerges the people generally resort to inherited habits, and traditional, prerevolutionary patterns of life reappear. The French Revolution passed through the three phases in a few years. The old patterns reappeared with Napoleon's counterrevolution in 1804 and the restoration of the Bourbons in 1815."

In recent times we have seen the same thing happen in Russia. There Stalin came to power and proceeded to purge the leadership in the same bloody manner that marked his rise to power. History again repeated itself in China as Mao Tse-tung recently ravaged the countryside with his Red Guards to remove "reactionary" elements. Today we hear another voice crying, "We are for spitting to killing, whatever is necessary to liberate us. . . . Our only problem now is to seize power . . . once you seize power, then you can talk about what system you'll use to maintain power." Is there any reason to suppose that their kind of power will accomplish anything?

While France was experiencing its bloody revolution, England was undergoing a different kind of revolution—a spiritual revolution—a revolution of love and reason. While Voltaire was cursing religion, William Wilberforce wrote that God had set before him two objects, "the suppression of the slave trade, and the reformation of manners." While guillotines were severing heads in Paris, petitions were being circulated in London to abolish slave trade. As a result of a spiritual revival of love and reason, England maintained its freedom from tyranny and reached its peak under Queen Victoria, while France floundered under a succession of monarchs and dictators.

To the famous British historian George M. Trevelyan, the British abolition movement was a turning point of history. He wrote that if the slave trade and slavery had not been brought to an end by the Christian abolitionists, the Industrial Revolution would have made Africa a great slave farm in the twentieth century and slavery would have wrecked civilization in Europe, Africa, and North America. Elie Halévy was of the opinion that abolition was first and foremost a Christian movement. This happened as a result of the spiritual awakening which God produced through the preaching and teaching of John Wesley and his colleagues.

The Clapham Sect, a group of businessmen and politicians, which led the movement, was advised by John Venn, a leading clergyman and founder of the Church Missionary Society. William Wilberforce, John Newton, T. Fowell Buxton, the three key leaders, were men converted through the impact of the movement. Of the petition presented in Parliament in 1796, 229,426 of the 358,852 signatures were those of Christians who were called Methodists. As a result there was a balance between political leadership and a vast concerned populace which supported the measures.

Constructive Revolution

Revolution based upon force and fear does not deal with the basic problems which face our generation. The solution must begin where the problem begins—with the individual, not with the masses. "The machine, be it mechanical, social, or economic, is neutral. In itself it neither imperils nor favors the flowering of personhood. That flowering is an interior, spiritual event," to use the words of Paul Tournier, Swiss physician and clinical psychologist.

Individuals make up society, and society cannot be changed until individuals are changed. Selfishness, prejudice, hate, greed, lust, are all individual problems which become the problems of collective man and society as a whole. Our problem is solved, then, if the individual is changed, that is, if enough individuals are changed. That is exactly what happened in the first century when a handful of the followers of Jesus started a spiritual revolution that changed the course of history.

J. B. Phillips, the famous translator, author, and authority on the history of the church, wrote in his translation of the book of Acts, *The Young Church in Action*, "It is a matter of sober historical fact that never before has any small body of people so moved the world that their enemies could say with tears of rage in their eyes that these men 'have turned the world upside down.'

"In the pages of this unpretentious second book (the book of Acts), written by the author of this third Gospel, the fresh air of Heaven is plainly blowing. . . . The Holy Spirit has a way of short-circuiting human problems. Indeed, in exactly the same way as Jesus Christ in the flesh cut right through the matted layers of tradition and exposed the real issue; just as He again and again brought down a theoretical problem to a personal issue, so we find here the Spirit of Jesus dealing not so much with problems as with people.

Many problems comparable to modern complexities never arise here because the men and women concerned were of one heart and mind in the Spirit. Many another issue is never allowed to arise because these early Christians were led by the Spirit to the main task of bringing people to God through Christ and were not permitted to enjoy fascinating sidetracks. One can hardly avoid concluding, since God's Holy Spirit cannot conceivably have changed one iota through the centuries, that He is perfectly prepared to short-circuit, by an inflow of love, wisdom, and understanding, many human problems today."

A careful study of the impact of first-century, classical Christianity caused Benjamin Franklin to insist, "He who introduces into public affairs the principles of primitive Christianity will change the face of the world."

First Century Revolution

First-century Christians, as exemplified by the Apostle Paul, were the original revolutionists. They had made the remarkable discovery that man could know God personally and experience His love and forgiveness, His purpose and peace and power for daily living. They believed that God had come to earth in the Person of Jesus of Nazareth in fulfillment of prophecies recorded in the Old Testament hundreds of years before He was born. They believed that He lived the most perfect life ever lived, taught as no one had ever taught, performed miracles, and died on the cross for the sins of man, in fulfillment of these same prophecies. Further, they believed that Jesus was actually raised from the dead and literally had come to dwell within them in His resurrected life and power. Through this intimate personal relationship with God in Christ, their lives were changed, as Paul describes: "When someone becomes a Christian he becomes a brand new person inside. He is not the same any more. A new life has begun! All these things are from God who brought us back to Himself through what Christ Jesus did. And God has given us the privilege of urging everyone to come into His favor."[1]

So great was their joy over this discovery that they went forth boldly into a hostile world that had crucified their Lord to proclaim His resurrection and the good news of God's love and forgiveness through His death on the cross. They did so at the risk of their lives, and tens of thousands died as martyrs to proclaim this revolutionary new truth.

Dedication—Essential Ingredient

Nechayev, a Marxist of the last century, who died in prison for his role in the assassination of Czar Alexander II, said, "The revolutionary man is a consecrated man. He has neither his own interest nor concerns nor feelings, no attachments nor property, not even a name. All for him is absorbed in the single exclusive interest, in the one thought, in the one passion–revolution."

But this quality of dedication was not original with the Marxists or communists of today. It was Jesus who said: "If any one desires to be My disciple, let him deny himself–that is, disregard, lose sight of and forget himself and his own interests–and take up his cross and follow Me (. . . conform wholly to My example in living and if need be in dying also)."[2]

This means that the one who wishes to follow Him as His disciple must be willing to forfeit all claim to his life and make Christ and His kingdom paramount in all of his consideration. That the Apostle Paul had done this, along with multiplied thousands of other Christians, is apparent as he refers to himself in the first chapter of the book of Romans as a "bondslave of Jesus." Later, Paul wrote, "I have been crucified with Christ: and I myself no longer live, but Christ lives in me. And the real life I now have within this body is a result of my trusting in the Son of God, who loved me and gave Himself for me."[3]

You Must Make Your Choice

Every inhabitant of this globe is involved in worldwide revolution. Every man must choose whether he will support, either actively or passively, revolution of force and fear or a revolution of love and reason. Dag Hammarskjold, former secretary general of the United Nations, emphasized the importance of the latter solution. Shortly before he was killed while on a peace mission to the Belgian Congo, he said, "I see no hope for world peace. We have tried so hard and failed so miserably. Unless the world has a spiritual rebirth within the next few years, civilization is doomed." That rebirth is to be found in Jesus Christ.

[1] II Corinthians 5:17-18, *Living New Testament*
[2] Matthew 16:24, *Amplified Bible*
[3] Galatians 2:20, LNT

Chapter 2

The Greatest Revolutionary

While visiting one of America's leading universities, I was invited to interview a well-known communist and professing atheist.

"Who, in your opinion," I asked, "is the most revolutionary person the world has ever known? Who has accomplished the most good for mankind throughout the centuries?"

From the expression and response it was obvious that such a question had never been considered before. After several moments of deliberation, "I guess I would have to say Jesus," was the reluctant reply. Through the years in many lands, I have asked these questions of knowledgeable people of all major religions. Their answers without exception have been, "Jesus of Nazareth." These questions are of utmost importance because there can be no true revolution without a qualified leader. Mob violence can be produced by agitators, but it results only in destruction. Well-motivated community renewal projects, on the other hand, can change a garbage-covered lot into a recreation area, but will black and white children play together there?

Radical revolutionaries disdain status quo and seek to destroy it. Many sincere community leaders in government and social service recognize the same ills and are also aware of the danger of a universal holocaust, and are attempting to extinguish the fire.

Both fail in bringing real solutions because both the revolutionary and the "community action" leader deal only with symptoms—not with causes. They may destroy the symptoms, they may change the symptoms, but the same inequalities and injustices only arise on the ruins of that which has been burned, or on the new playground that has been created.

Both are right in their desire: they see the need for change and they are not satisfied to sit idly by. But their so-called revolution is no revolution at all because the leaders of both courses fail to deal with the inner man. Only one revolutionary throughout the whole of history has dealt with that problem. That revolutionary is Jesus Christ.

Must we be saddled with these half-solutions? No! We can participate now in a revolution that goes beyond the symptoms and deals with man's root problem.

A World-Changing Leader

One author writes of Jesus, "Nineteen centuries have come and gone, and today He is the centerpiece of the human race and the leader of the column of progress. I am far within the mark when I say that all the armies that ever marched and all the navies that were ever built and all the parliaments that ever sat, and all the kings that ever reigned put together have not affected the life of man upon this earth as has that one solitary life."

Wherever the true message of Jesus Christ has gone, new life, new hope, new purpose for living have been the results. Let us consider why, without fear of contradiction, He can be called "History's Greatest Revolutionary." Indeed, everything about Him was revolutionary: His birth, His life, His teachings, His miracles, His death, His resurrection.

Prophecies of His Visit to Earth Were Revolutionary

Jesus of Nazareth was born almost 2000 years ago. For hundreds of years the great prophets of Israel had foretold His coming. The Old Testament, which was written by many individuals over a period of 1,500 years, contains over 300 references concerning Jesus. For hundreds of years the scholars of Israel looked forward to the coming of their Messiah.

For example, over 400 years before His birth, the prophet Micah foretold the precise location of that event: "As for you, Bethlehem Ephrathah, little as you are among the thousands of Judah, from you shall He come forth to Me, who is to be ruler over Israel. His goings forth are from of old, from days of eternity."[1]

Thus when King Herod inquired of the priests and scribes where their Messiah was to be born, they replied, "In Bethlehem of Judea, for so it is written by the prophet . . ."[2]

His Birth Was Unique and Revolutionary

Through the centuries man has demanded signs that would enable him to discern what was true. God promised that the people could know when the true Son of God had appeared: "Therefore the Lord himself shall give you a sign; Behold, a virgin shall conceive, and bear a son, and shall call his name Immanuel."[3]

In making his written report concerning the life of Jesus, Matthew emphasized the revolutionary manner by which Jesus Christ entered into human life: a virgin birth. This supernatural birth set the stage for His perfect life of righteousness before God and man.

His Childhood Was Revolutionary

Though little is recorded of the childhood of Jesus, what is known of His early years suggests a young life that is without parallel in the life of man upon the earth.

As a boy, during an annual family trip to Jerusalem, Jesus slipped away alone and went up to the temple. While there, He engaged several learned men in discussion, answering their questions and challenging their thinking with questions of His own. "And all that heard him were astonished at his understanding and answers."[4] After three days of diligent search, His parents found Him and asked for an explanation of His absence. Jesus' answer at age 12 announced the very purpose for His life upon earth. "Why is it that you were looking for Me?" He said. "Did you not know that I must be about My Father's business?"

His Teachings Were Revolutionary

The teachings of Jesus Christ were revolutionary. They are still changing the course of events today. Those who listened to Him said, "Never man spake like this man." He said things that men had never thought or spoken before. His emphasis on God's love for man, and His command for man to love God and his fellowman as himself, were revolutionary. God loves us when we are good or when we are bad, but Christ came to die to make us good in God's sight.

Without question, the greatest teaching of Jesus was that salvation comes not by what man does for God, but by what God does for man through His Son. A group of people approached Christ and inquired, "What shall we do, that we might work the works of God?" Jesus replied, "This is the work of God, that ye believe on Him whom He (God) hath sent."[6] "Unless you believe that I am who I am, you will die in your sins."[7]

A Revolutionary Salvation

Salvation by faith, not works, is revolutionary because every religion of the world, except Christianity, teaches that man must seek to find God and earn his salvation by good deeds. Jesus repeatedly emphasized good works, but never as a means to salvation. Rather, the Bible teaches, good works are produced in and through us by the Holy Spirit after man believes. The Apostle Paul emphasized this fact when he explained, "For by grace you have been saved through faith; and that not of yourselves, it is the gift of God; not as a result of works, that no one should boast. For we are His workmanship, created in Christ Jesus for good works, which God prepared beforehand, that we should walk in them."[8]

Eternal life—salvation—is the result of receiving a gift, God's Son, and is not ours because we have earned it. Jesus explains, "For God loved the world so much that He *gave* His only Son so that everyone who believes on Him should not be lost, but should have eternal life."[9] One cannot pay for a gift. One simply accepts it and says "thank you" to the giver.

His Miracles Were Revolutionary

In addition to the revolutionary message He proclaimed, the miracles Jesus performed stand as a testimony to His true person. They were not capricious demonstrations of brute power, but were acts of a loving God, anxious to reveal His benevolent character to man.

The crowds watched in amazement as He demonstrated His miracle-performing love. "He does all things well," they exclaimed.

Even today, people in Tiberias believe in His miracles. When I was boating on the Sea of Galilee, I inquired of one of the leading citizens there, "Do you believe that Jesus fed the multitude of five thousand with five loaves and two fishes?"

"Of course, I believe," he replied.

After recording the changing of water into wine, the healing of the centurion's servant, the healing of a man paralyzed for thirty-eight years, the giving of sight to a man born blind, the raising of Lazarus from the dead, John, the apostle who had seen all these miracles performed, wrote, "But these (things are) written, that ye might believe that Jesus is the Christ, the Son of God; and that believing ye might have life through His name."[10]

His Death and Resurrection Were Revolutionary

Imagine any one predicting accurately his own death and resurrection! And yet this is exactly what Jesus Christ did. He foretold, "The Son of man must suffer many things, and be rejected of the elders and chief priests and scribes, and be slain, and be raised the third day."[11]

In fact the priests and scribes knew this and attempted to prevent its occurrence by placing guards at the tomb. But no human effort could prevent what God had planned.

Professor Edwin Selwyn, in his work, *The Approach to Christianity,* said, "The fact that Christ rose from the dead on the third day in full continuity of body and soul, and passed into a mode of new relationships with those who knew Him on earth—that fact seems as secure as historical evidence can make it."

The death and resurrection of Jesus Christ was the message of the revolutionary New Testament Church. It is a revolutionary message today. It is a fact of history.

Not only were Jesus' death and resurrection revolutionary, but so was the purpose for which they occurred. Jesus Christ was the only Man in all of history who was born to die. By dying on the cross for our sins He willingly took upon Himself the death that each individual person deserves because of sin. It is by believing that Jesus Christ died for man—by receiving Him personally—that one becomes a Christian.

His Influence through the Centuries Has Been Revolutionary

Moments before Jesus physically ascended into heaven, He issued to His followers the Great Commission: "Go ye therefore, and teach all nations, baptizing them in the name of the Father, and of the Son, and of the Holy Ghost: teaching them to observe all things whatsoever I have commanded you: and, lo, I am with you alway, even unto the end of the world."[12]

Beginning in Jerusalem, the early Christians took His message to the ends of the then-known world, so that before many years had passed, even the enemies of the faith admitted, "These that have turned the world upside down are come hither also."[13] Like begets like. And history's greatest Revolutionary has produced some of the most revolutionary men of all time and started the greatest possible revolution, the changing of the lives of men.

The British scholar W. H. Griffith Thomas said, "The testimony to the present work of Jesus Christ is no less real than it has been in the past. In the case of all the other great names of the world's history, the inevitable and invariable experience has been that the particular man is first a power, then only a name, and last of all a mere memory. Of Jesus Christ the exact opposite is true. He died on a cross of shame, His name gradually became more and more powerful, and He is the greatest influence in the world today. There is, as has been well said, a fifth gospel being written—

the work of Jesus Christ in the hearts and lives of men and nations.

"The present social status of men, women, and children is so familiar to us that we sometimes fail to realize what it was before Christ came. In the Roman world the father had absolute right over his children to sell, to enslave, to kill them. It is Christianity that has made these atrocities impossible. Woman was the living chattel of her husband, as she is still in some parts of the world. It is through Christianity that she has obtained a new status, and now in Christian countries 'Home' receives its true and full meaning. The slavery of the Roman Empire was one of its most deep-seated features, and the power of master over slave was absolute and was often exercised with cruelty and ferocity. But Christianity proclaimed the universality and brotherhood of all men in Christ, and thereby struck at the root of slavery, and wherever the gospel of Christ has had its way, slavery has been compelled to disappear."

Caleb Cushing, statesman, and former Attorney General of the United States, suggests: "The Christian religion levels upward, elevating all men to the same high standard of sanctity, faith and spiritual promise on earth as in heaven. Just so is it, that wherever Christianity is taught, it inevitably dignifies and exalts the female character."

George Romanes, the British physicist, made this statement: "It is on all sides worth considering (blatant ignorance or base vulgarity alone excepted) that the revolution effected by Christianity in human life is immeasurable and unparalleled by any other movement in history.

"But not only is Christianity thus so immeasurably in advance of all other religions. It is no less so of every other system of thought that has ever been promulgated in regard to all that is moral and spiritual. Whether it be true or false, it is certain that neither philosophy, science, nor poetry has ever produced results in thought, conduct, or beauty in any degree to be compared with it.

"Only to a man wholly destitute of spiritual perception can it be that Christianity should fail to appear the greatest exhibition of the beautiful, the sublime, and of all else that appeals to our spiritual nature, which has ever been known upon our earth."

Kenneth Scott Latourette, director of the department of religion in Yale's graduate school, historian, and author of a set of well-known works, *Expansion of Christianity*, comments: "Measured by its fruits in the human race, that short life has been the most influential ever lived on this planet. As we have been at pains to point out, the impress of that life, far from fading with the passing centuries, has deepened. Through Him millions of individuals have been transformed and have begun to live the kind of life which He exemplified. Gauged by the consequences which have followed, the birth, life, death and resurrection of Jesus have been the most important events in the history of man. Measured by His influence, Jesus is central in the human story."

Ernst Haeckel, the noted German scientist and philosopher, who was an untiring protagonist of atheistic rationalism, admitted the world-transforming power of the Bible when he said: "Beyond all doubt the present degree of human culture owes, in great part, its perfection to the propagation of the Christian system of morals and its ennobling influence."

His Claims Were Revolutionary

Jesus claimed to be God. He said, "I and My Father are one. . . . he that hath seen Me hath seen the Father."[14] Who but Jesus would dare to claim, "I am the way, the truth and the life; no one comes to the Father, but through Me"?

Either Jesus of Nazareth was who He claimed to be, the Son of God, the Savior of mankind, or He was the greatest impostor the world has ever known. Since He has accomplished more good for mankind than anyone who has ever lived, if His claims are false, a lie has accomplished more good than has the truth.

Are you interested in revolution? Do you want to help change the world? We invite you to join with us in following the Greatest Revolutionary of the centuries. He is alive and waiting to show you His peerless plan for your life.

[1] Micah 5:2, *Berkeley*
[2] Matthew 2:4-6, *Berkeley*
[3] Isaiah 7:14
[4] Luke 2:47
[5] Luke 2:49
[6] John 6:29
[7] John 8:24, *Phillips*
[8] Ephesians 2:8-10, NAS
[9] John 3:16, *Phillips*
[10] John 20:31
[11] Luke 9:22, *LNT*
[12] Matthew 28:19,20
[13] Acts 17:6
[14] John 10:30; 14:9

Chapter 3

The Revolutionary Offer

Movements and ideologies of many varieties are attempting to manipulate a revolutionary encounter with this generation; and this generation is seeking an encounter with the society in which it finds itself. There are many young and sincere leaders who believe that bequeathed to this generation is the challenge to break the barriers of war, race, poverty, to "make it go right," to solve the complexities of a world out of gear.

Those of this new generation have a strong desire to change society. They say, "We want badly to have an impact on the society in which we live." Technology and science, as we look forward, have a bright future, and yet, if we look at ourselves socially and are realistic concerning the future there is room only for disillusionment or discouragement.

Thoreau said, "The mass of men lead lives of quiet desperation." We are in danger of deceiving ourselves as we say that man will work it out all right, for, as we scan the pages of history, doubts arise.

The common denominator of young and old seems to be disillusionment. They have goals, but no purpose. They have spokes but no hub. In education and in business, they are learning how to make a living, but not how to live. One man said, "I've tried everything that life has to offer, but all I see is one guy trying to outdo another in a futile attempt at happiness."

Many of our leaders have come to the conclusion that we may be writing the last chapter of history. The late Sir Winston Churchill said, "This generation has placed the world on trial for its life, and may well live to see the end of civilization as we know it."

As much as for scholarly, athletic or political ability, respect is held for the man who is open and honest. By and large, today's young person is more honest in saying what he thinks and feels concerning his likes and dislikes.

"Tell it like it is" is the standard plea for honesty. So what is the solution? What is the answer that will change a sick, reeling world—that will provide an antidote for the inherited and self-made ills of man? Will man, through self-effort and social reform, eventually emerge free from the entrapments and hangups of the past into a bright, light future? History tells us no.

There is a way out, however. The answer is given by millions of individuals who have chosen to follow Jesus Christ and have encountered Him in a personal way.

Dr. Charles Malik, internationally recognized scholar and statesman, former president of the General Assembly of the United Nations, and now professor of philosophy at the American University in Beirut, Lebanon, represents their solution with these words: "It is perfectly clear that we could save nobody and nothing if we are not first sure of ourselves. Only those who stay close to Jesus Christ can help others who are far away. Only those who prefer Him to everything else, even the call of the needy world, can be used of Him for the need of the world. Nothing, therefore, is more necessary than to arouse responsible Christians from their lethargy and slumber into both the infinite dangers and the infinite possibilities of the moment." This brilliant man from Lebanon, a great scholar and leader in the affairs of nations, goes on to say, "The heart of the whole matter is faith in Jesus Christ. Do we believe in Him as passionately as others believe in their own ideas and systems? If we do, then we ought to do better than they, for we worship a person; they worship an idea. We worship life and strength and love and victory; they worship negation and hatred. Christ can do without us—and He may be doing so already in the vast spaces of Asia and Africa —and if we fail Him, it cannot be that He failed us; we will only have proven that we are unprofitable servants."

There are many things that Jesus offers to do for you individually that no one else can do. In this chapter I want to concentrate on four definite things and then share with you how you can encounter Christ personally in your life. First, He is the only one who can *pardon* man from his sin. Second, He alone can give *purpose* for life. Third, He alone can give *peace* to a troubled heart. Fourth, only Jesus can give you *power* to live an abundant life.

Pardon from Sin

First of all, then, Jesus is the only One who offers to pardon man from his sin. It is written in the Bible that God is holy and man is sinful and that there is a great gulf between the two, which man cannot bridge, no matter how good he is. The Bible says that all have sinned and come short of the glory of God and that the wages of sin is death—eternal separation from God; but the gift of God is eternal life through Jesus Christ our Lord.

It is also written, "God so greatly loved and dearly prized the world that He (even) gave up His only begotten [unique] Son, so that whoever believes in . . . Him may not perish . . . but have eternal [everlasting] life."[1] God bridges the chasm to man through His Son, Jesus Christ.

Sin Defined

Now, let us consider for a moment what we mean by sin. Sin is not necessarily a matter of lying, stealing or being immoral. Basically, sin is an attitude of independence from God. Man was created to have fellowship with God, but, because of his stubborn self-will, he chose to go his own independent way, thus fellowship with God was broken. This self-will, characterized by an attitude of active rebellion or passive indifference, is an evidence of what the Bible calls sin. Sin is an act of going one's own independent way. It is a lack of relationship or fellowship with God. The Bible clearly defines sin as falling short of God's standard, which is His own perfect righteousness. Sin manifests itself as self-centeredness.

There is a throne in your life, and either you are on the throne or Jesus Christ is on that throne. If you say, "I am the master of my life; I will do as I please," self is on the throne. On the other hand, according to the epistle of John, Chapter 1, if Christ is on the throne, you will enjoy wonderful fellowship with Him, and His blood will cleanse and keep on cleansing you from all sin.

Pull a lamp plug from an electric outlet and contact with the current is broken—the light goes out. Push the plug into the outlet again, and the light goes on. The current is constant—the plug is the variable.

Man can be compared to that plug. Because we do not have fellowship with God, we walk in darkness—we have chosen to go our own way. This is what the Bible calls sin.

Provision Made for Sin

Now, what is God's provision for sin? In the Old Testament, animals were brought to the priest by the Israelites as sacrifices for sin. These animals had to be perfect, without spot or blemish, and the sin of the one making the sacrifice was transferred to the innocent offering. The animal was slain and its blood was sprinkled on the altar by the priest as a temporary covering for the individual's sins.

This is a picture of the coming of God's one special Lamb, whose blood would not cover man's sins just temporarily but would wash them away forever. God sent His only Son, who was without sin, the Lamb of God, without spot or blemish, to give His life, to shed

His blood upon the cross for the forgiveness of our sins.

"Without the shedding of blood," we are told in the Scriptures, "there is no forgiveness of sins."[2] There is no more precious truth in the word of God than this, that Christ died for our sins.

As one studies the religions of the world, one becomes aware that no provision is made for the forgiveness of sin apart from the cross of Jesus Christ. Basically, man subscribes to the concept that if his good works outweigh his bad works, he will go to heaven or the equivalent. But if his bad works outweigh his good works, he will go to hell or the equivalent—according to his particular religion.

Of course, he does not know until this life is over to which place he will go. What a tragedy! How inadequate is such a religion or philosophy. God has promised that we can know Him and have fellowship with Him for all eternity, through His Son, the Lord Jesus Christ.

At the conclusion of one of my university lectures on "The Uniqueness of Jesus," a young Hindu professor from India approached me. He was very angry and impatient. "I resent you Christians," he said, "I resent the arrogance with which you say that you have the only way to God. I believe that Christianity is one way, but only one way. Hinduism is another. Buddhism, Shintoism and other religions are all ways to God," he protested.

I reminded him of the writings of the great Hindu leader, Mahatma Gandhi, who, in spite of all his devotion to his religion, stated in his autobiography: "It is a constant torture to me that I am still so far from Him whom I know to be my very life and being. I know it is my wretchedness and wickedness that keeps me from Him." The Hindu replied that he had once believed that Mr. Gandhi was God, but, of course, he no longer believed this.

As we talked I discovered that this young man was unusually brilliant. He was completing double doctorates—one in physics and one in chemistry—at the same time. As we talked he began to see that Christianity is uniquely different.

He saw that Christianity is not just another man-made religion or philosophy, but that it makes provision for man's basic need, which is forgiveness of sin. Soon he admitted that, although he was a devout follower of his religion—diligent in the reading of the sacred Hindu writings and in all of the ritual of his faith—he had never found God.

I called his attention to the difference in the lives of his Christian friends. He admitted that they had something that he did not have. It was obvious that "that something" was the living Savior who had come to live within them and had forgiven them of their sins. Soon we were on our knees together and this young Hindu prayed that Jesus would forgive his sins and become his Savior.

Take Buddha out of Buddhism, Mohammed out of Islam, and, in like manner, the founders of various other religions out of their religions, and little would be changed; but take Christ out of Christianity and there would be nothing left, for Christianity is not a philosophy, nor a code of ethics, nor a way of life—it is a personal relationship with a living Savior.

Jesus Gives Purpose to Life

Not only is Jesus of Nazareth unique in that He is the only One who offers to pardon our sins, but He is the only One who offers to give purpose for life.

Let us consider God's purpose for men. One can readily see that God has created everything for a purpose. The Bible says that it was through the Son that God made the whole universe, and to the Son He has ordained that all creation shall ultimately belong. There is order, system, and design to the whole of creation. Man is the highest expression of God's creation. God created man with a free will, with a right of choice. Man can say "yes" or "no" to God, and for the most part, he has chosen to say "no." Because of this tragedy, those who have said "no" have never discovered God's purpose for their lives. When one says "yes" to Christ, he comes into an assurance and knowledge of God's purpose for him. "The steps of a good man are ordered by the Lord." "All things work together for good to them that love God, to them who are the called according to His purpose."[3]

There are great benefits to be derived from being where God wants you to be and doing what He wants you to do.

Consider marriage, for example. Did you know that, according to Dr. Pitirim Sorokin, a famous Harvard professor, one out of two and one-half marriages in this country ends in divorce? Yet, where the husband and wife are Christians, and have a family altar, where they read the Bible and pray together daily, only one out of 1,015 marriages in this country ends in divorce.

Jesus Christ makes the difference. He brings real purpose to marriage. In view of the facts, is it reasonable to gamble on marriage without Christ?

You may say, "I don't understand how Christ can make such a great difference." The answer is simple. There is a throne in your life. If you are on that throne, your ego and the ego of the one whom you marry will war against each other, and friction is inevitable. However, if Christ is on the throne of the lives of both husband and wife, He will not war against Himself and there will be peace.

Men who do not know Christ and plan their lives without Him become like a ship without a rudder and without sail, drifting with the tide upon a rough sea.

Material Success Not Enough

For example, in 1923 a very important meeting was held at the Edgewater Beach Hotel in Chicago. Attending this meeting were nine of the world's most successful financiers: Charles Schwab, steel magnate; Samuel Insull, president of the largest utility company; Howard Hopson, president of the largest gas company; Arthur Cotton, the greatest wheat speculator; Richard Whitney, president of the New York stock exchange; Albert Fall, a member of the President's Cabinet; Leon Fraser, president of the Bank of International Settlements; Jesse Livermore, the great "bear" on Wall Street; and Ivar Krueger, head of the most powerful monopoly.

Twenty-five years later, Charles Schwab had died in bankruptcy, having lived on borrowed money for five years before his death; Samuel Insull had died a fugitive from justice, and penniless in a foreign land; Howard Hopson was insane; Arthur Cotton had died abroad, insolvent; Richard Whitney had spent time in Sing Sing; Albert Fall had been pardoned so that he could die at home; Jesse Livermore, Ivar Krueger and Leon Fraser had all died by suicide. All of these men had learned well the art of making a living, but none of them had learned **HOW TO LIVE!**

Successful Failures

H. G. Wells, famous historian and philosopher, said, at the age of 61, "I have no peace. All life is at the end of its tether."

The poet Byron said, "My days are in the yellow leaf, the flowers and fruits of life are gone, the worm and the canker, and the grief are mine alone."

Ralph Barton, one of the top cartoonists of the nation, left this note pinned to his pillow before taking his life: "I have had few difficulties, many friends, great success; I have gone from wife to wife, and from house to house, visited great countries of the world, but I am fed up with inventing devices to fill up 24 hours of the day."

Pascal, French physicist and philosopher, described the problem and solution this way: "There is a God-shaped vacuum in the heart of every man which cannot be filled by any created thing, but only by God the Creator, made known through Jesus Christ." St. Augustine said centuries ago, "Thou hast made us for Thyself, O God, and our hearts are restless until they find their rest in Thee."

Dare I say that there is a vacuum in your life and

a restlessness in your heart? I do not know you. I do not need to know you, but in all honesty, in the quiet of your own heart, if you do not know Jesus Christ, you are saying today, "Yes, there is a vacuum; I am not satisfied with my life."

You never will be satisfied until Christ shows you the very purpose for which He created you. No one else who ever lived, nor anything else, can do this—no man, no religion, no philosophy. Jesus said, "I am the way, the truth and the life; no man cometh unto the Father, but by Me."

Jesus Alone Can Give You Peace

Jesus alone offers pardon for our sins. Jesus alone offers purpose for life. Jesus of Nazareth, the Prince of Peace, is the only One who offers to give you peace. As someone said, "There will never be peace in the individual heart or at the peace tables of the world until the Prince of peace reigns supreme in the hearts of men." Jesus said, "Peace I leave with you, My peace I give unto you; not as the world giveth, give I unto you. Let not your heart be troubled, neither let it be afraid."[4] He also said, "Come unto Me, all ye that labor and are heavy laden, and I will give you rest."[5]

The Christian is not exempt from problems. Becoming a Christian does not mean that you will suddenly be ushered into a utopian situation, but rather that you have One with you who said, "Lo, I am with you all the days—perpetually, uniformly and on every occasion—to the (very) close and consummation of the age."[6] "I will never leave you, nor forsake you."[7] "My peace I give you."[8]

From Tragedy to Triumph

At the presidential prayer breakfast which is sponsored by the International Christian Leadership Conference in Washington, D. C., under whose sponsorship I was speaking, I encountered a young Naval Commander who was a fraternity brother and had been a debate colleague of mine during college days.

A tragedy had recently taken place in his life through the loss of a child, and he asked if I would come and talk with him and his heartbroken wife.

As we talked together that evening, both my friend and his wife invited Jesus Christ to be their Savior and Lord. As Christ came into their lives, their lives were changed, and they experienced a wonderful peace. The following year, I again met this friend under the same circumstances and learned that, shortly after our first visit, another of his children had become ill and died. Cancer of the nervous system had resulted in her death. The finest of medical attention had been provided, but to no avail.

He had loved his daughter dearly, and now she was gone. But I shall never forget that day as with heartwarming smile he said, "Though I do not understand it, as dearly as we loved our little girl and as much as we hated to see her go, during the time of her illness and after she was gone, the presence of the Lord Jesus Christ has been so very real. Through it all we have had a peace that is indescribable."

Tragedy, heartache and sorrow will come into your life, too: but Christ, the Prince of peace, wants to take control of your life—to give you His pardon, His purpose and His peace.

Jesus Gives Power

In addition to His offer of pardon, purpose and peace, Jesus of Nazareth is also the only One who offers to give you power to live a revolutionary new life.

Frequently men and women will say, "I would like to become a Christian, but if I do, I am sure that I will never be able to live the life. You don't know the mistakes that I have made, the resentments that I have, my tendencies to sin, my immorality, heavy drinking, my dependence upon drugs, my cruel tongue and many, many other problems. I do not believe that I could live the Christian life." But, as they have given their lives to Christ, these same people have discovered that the Christian life is a supernatural life. Jesus Christ literally comes to live within us. Therefore, it is no longer what we do but what He does, because He is the One who provides the power and we are merely the instruments through whom He releases that power.

One night, a man named Nicodemus—a very good, moral, ethical, religious leader, and a ruler of the Jews, came to see Jesus and asked, "Rabbi (meaning Teacher), we know that you are a teacher come from God: for no man can do these miracles that you do except God be with him."[9] Jesus answered, "I say unto you, except a man be born again, he cannot see the kingdom of God."[10]

Nicodemus did not know what He meant. He said, "Do you mean that I must enter my mother's womb the second time to be born?" Jesus said, "No, you are born once in the flesh, but in order to enter the kingdom of God you must be born of the Spirit." We are born with a physical body to live on a physical plane; but the kingdom of God is a spiritual kingdom and God is a spiritual Being. If we are to have fellowship with Him, we must become spiritual creatures through a spiritual birth.

Picture a caterpillar—just an ugly, hairy worm—crawling in the dirt. If you could communicate with it, you might say, "Why do you crawl in the dirt? Why don't you fly like the butterfly?" No doubt it would reply, "It is impossible for me to fly for I am earth-bound; I can only crawl in the dust."

Then you would suggest, "We will attach some butterfly wings to your body." "No, that would do no good," would be the reply. Then you would ask, "Why don't you take a course in aviation, and then you would be able to fly?" But all of this would be to no avail.

So it is with people who try to become Christians by good works—such as good conduct, church attendance, reading the Bible, praying, etc.—rather than by way of the new birth, as Jesus commanded.

One day the caterpillar weaves about its body a cocoon and later out of that cocoon there emerges a beautiful butterfly. We do not understand fully what has taken place. We know only that where a worm once crawled in the dust a butterfly now soars in the heavens. So it is in the life of a Christian, this new birth takes place when Jesus of Nazareth, the risen Lord and Savior, comes to live within you.

If you have not already received Christ as your Savior and Lord, will you in the quiet of this moment, receive Him as your Savior—invite Him to come into your life to live His life in you, to pardon your sin, to give purpose to your life, to give you His peace and power? If this is your desire, why not bow your head right now and pray this prayer: "Lord Jesus, come into my life. Pardon my sin. I surrender my will, the throne of my life, to You. Show me Your purpose for my life and I will do it. Give me Your peace and power that I may please and honor You, Lord Jesus. Amen." Remember, God honors the attitude of your heart—not the words of your prayer. If you genuinely desire to receive Christ, He will come into your life.

Adventure with Christ

As you receive Christ into your life, you begin the great adventure for which He created you. We are told in the Bible, "God has given us eternal life, and this life is in His Son. He who has the Son has life."[11] When you receive Christ, you have eternal life here and now. As you continue in obedience to His commands, you will experience the fulfillment of His promise of an abundant life.

[1] John 3:16, *Amplified Bible*
[2] Hebrews 9:22, NAS
[3] Romans 8:28
[4] John 14:27
[5] Matthew 11:28
[6] Matthew 28:20, *Amplified Bible*
[7] Hebrews 13:5
[8] John 14:27, NAS
[9] John 3:2
[10] John 3:3
[11] I John 5:11,12

Chapter 4

The Intellectual Meets the Revolutionary

At twelve years of age Jesus amazed the greatest intellectuals of His nation with His knowledge and wisdom. He had no college degrees, but leading philosophers were baffled by His wisdom and asked, "How can these things be?" In His teachings He gave flashing glimpses of His remarkable knowledge of meteorology, anatomy, biology and the other sciences. With no difficulty whatever, He unmasked the diabolically clever traps of His enemies. He answered the unspoken questions and revealed the unuttered scorn of His critics. The guards sent to arrest Him returned to their masters empty handed, their only excuse, "Never man spake like this man."

Jesus Christ was the intellectual's Intellectual. Not only did He change the course of time and history, He also changed the channels of human knowledge. The intellectual revolution which He began shattered the bondage of tradition and opened the doors of knowledge to the poor, the underprivileged, and the minorities, as well as to the intellectuals.

One such intellectual was Lew Wallace, a famous literary critic, and a general during the Civil War in the United States. He was a friend of the famous skeptic Robert Ingersoll. They were both antagonistic to Christianity and religion of all forms. They believed Christianity kept men in ignorance, fear, superstition and bondage. One Sunday morning as he and Ingersoll were riding on a train they decided, as they saw many people going to Sunday worship, that these people needed to be enlightened—they needed to be liberated from their bondage of superstition. And so they agreed that they would do special research and write a book that would forever liberate Christian people from their ignorance and superstition. Mr. Wallace accepted the responsibility. For two years he studied in the leading libraries of Europe and America doing research for this book that would "forever liberate the masses from their ignorance and superstition, from this myth of Christianity." He finished his study and began to write. He wrote his first chapter and as he was laboring over his second chapter, suddenly he found himself on his knees saying, "My Lord and my God." The One whom he had set out to disprove, had captured him. This man, Lew Wallace, became one of the devout followers of Christ and authored that great Christian classic, *Ben Hur*.

The Tragedy of Ignorance

J. B. Phillips, in his preface to *The Young Church in Action*, speaks of the tragedy of spiritual ignorance of many intellectuals. "It is one of the curious phenomena of modern times that it is considered perfectly respectable to be abysmally ignorant of the Christian faith. Men and women who would be deeply ashamed of having their ignorance exposed in matters of poetry, music, or painting, for example, are not in the least perturbed to be found ignorant of the New Testament. Indeed it is perfectly obvious from the remarks sometimes made by intellectuals and from their own writings, that apart from half-remembered scraps left over from childhood's memory they have no knowledge of the New Testament at all. Very rarely does a man or woman give honest, intelligent, adult attention to the writings of the New Testament and then decide that Jesus was merely a misguided man. Even less frequently will he conclude that the whole Christian religion is founded upon a myth. The plain fact is not that men have given the New Testament their serious attention and found it spurious, but that they have never given it their serious attention at all. Let our intelligent men and women be urged, goaded, even shamed into reading this remarkable collection of early Christian literature for themselves. Let this ignorance of what Christianity teaches and practices be shown up for the intellectual affectation that it really is. Let the ill-informed critic of the Christian religion read particularly the Acts of the Apostles. Here is a simple, unvarnished, conscientious account of the behavior and actions of quite a small group of people who honestly believed that Jesus was right in His claims. Let the critics put aside for a moment their contempt for (and ignorance of) the Church as it is today, and let them feel afresh the astonishing impact of this tiny group of devoted men and women. Or let them read the letters of this same New Testament and see for themselves the new qualities of living which are taken almost as a matter of course in those human unselfconscious writings. No honest reader can evade the conclusion that something very powerful and very unusual has happened. People are unquestionably being changed at the root of their being: cowards become heroes; sinners are transformed; fear, greed, envy and pride are expelled by a flood of something above and beyond normal human experience. For in the pages of this New Testament the cruel, the wicked, the evil-minded and the God-less become filled with selfless love, with gay and generous courage. The critics of Christianity have got somehow to explain this. Moreover, within a couple of generations, or even less, the Message of Christ was being taken by devoted men and women to a good part of the then-known world. The new fellowship of those who knew God through Christ proved highly infectious and groups of (Christians) sprang up and flourished in the most unlikely places."

For more than 20 years I have worked with the so-called intelligentsia and have spoken to tens of thousands of collegians and professors on hundreds of campuses around the world. Yet, I have not met a single person in all these years who has said, "I have considered the historical evidence and the claims of Christ and I cannot believe that He is the Son of God." This may be illustrated through the life of a well-known scholar at one of our nation's leading seminaries. He did not believe in the deity of Christ, yet he has taught thousands of young ministers who fill the pulpits of our land. I was invited one day to visit with him in his office, by a friend of mine who was getting his doctorate under this great intellectual. My friend explained, "He does not believe what we believe. He is a good man. I like him. He is personable and warm-hearted. I think you might be able to communicate with him, so if you are interested, I would like for you to meet him." I was introduced as the president of Campus Crusade for Christ. His first words were, "Mr. Bright, when you talk to college students about becoming a Christian, what do you tell them?" Since I knew his reputation I did not want to respond without weighing my words carefully, and before I could reply, he asked a second question, "Better still, what would you tell me, if I would like to become a Christian?" I took him at his word, and drew a circle on a sheet of paper. In the circle I placed a throne and on the throne I placed the letter "E," representing ego or self. I said, "In order to become a Christian, one must surrender the control of his life to Christ. Christ must be on the throne as Lord and Savior." He replied, "That's my problem. Intellectual pride has kept me from doing this. Many honors have come to me in the academic realm, and I haven't been willing to humble myself before God." He continued, "Let me share with you some of my background. My father was a famous skeptic. He was a minister, but he denied the deity of Christ, and I grew up in that atmosphere. I have denied the deity of Christ all these years and have taught thousands of young men to do the same. But in recent times I have been reading the writings of the church fathers and the biographies of great men, such as John Wesley and St. Augustine. Now I am convinced, intellectually, that Jesus is the Son of God. But I do not know Him personally, as

John Wesley and St. Augustine knew Him as their personal Savior."

We were interrupted by a telephone call at that moment and, because of other scheduled appointments, there was no opportunity to finish our conversation. He asked if we could return two days later, which we did. We went into another office, where there were no telephones. He locked the door behind us, and said, "I want you to know that I went this morning to one of the local churches, took communion and prepared my heart for your coming. I have been reading and meditating on the third chapter of John with its teaching on a spiritual birth. I want you to pray for me that I may know Jesus as my personal Savior." I prayed, and then he prayed, and my friend prayed, and that day this man of international renown became as a little child and his life was changed. His teachings changed and his whole philosophy of life became different. He had encountered the greatest Revolutionary of all time. There have been other skeptics, some of them famous scholars, who have experienced this same revolutionary encounter with Christ.

Discovering Faith

Dr. C. E. M. Joad, one of the world's most famous philosophers, joined Bertrand Russell, H. G. Wells, and Bernard Shaw, his close friends, to work together to do everything they could to destroy the Christian faith. Dr. Joad had written several volumes in which he sought to undermine Christianity. Because of his great influence, the books he had written had a devastating impact. In 1948, I saw a picture of Dr. Joad inside the front cover of the magazine section of the Los Angeles Times. This venerable scholar was in his 70's. In the accompanying article, there was a statement by him which shocked the academic world. He wrote, "I have subscribed all my life to the life-force philosophy, which is: God is a part of the universe—should the universe be destroyed, God would be destroyed. I have ridiculed the idea of man's sin. I have believed that man is good; and that, given a little time, we would have heaven on earth. However, two world wars and the imminence of another have demonstrated conclusively to me that man is not good. Man is evil. The only explanation for man's sin is found in the Bible and the only solution for man's sin is found in the cross of Jesus Christ. The One whom I have denied all my life I must now embrace." Dr. Joad became a devout follower of Christ and I have in my library his last book, *My Return to Faith.* He had a revolutionary encounter with Christ.

Another typical skeptic was C. S. Lewis, one of Oxford University's most famous professors. For years he was an agnostic who denied the deity of Christ. Later he became a devout follower of Christ and wrote many outstanding books advocating belief in Him as Savior.

In *The Case for Christianity,* Mr. Lewis states: "A man who was merely a man and said the sort of things Jesus said wouldn't be a great moral teacher. He would either be a lunatic on the level with a man who says he's a poached egg—or else he would be the devil of hell; you must take your choice. Either this was, and is, the Son of God, or else a madman or something worse. You can shut Him up for a demon; or you can fall at His feet and call Him Lord and God. But don't come up with any patronizing nonsense about His being a great moral teacher. He hasn't left that alternative open to us."

To some of my readers these stories may sound incredible. Yet, millions of people through the centuries have been changed through a revolutionary encounter with Jesus Christ, history's most revolutionary Person. Among these are thousands of students and professors who are committing their lives to Jesus Christ on college campuses around the world.

They Say It As It Is

Charlie Powell, while student body president at the University of California at Berkeley, made his commitment to Christ during the early stage of the free speech movement. "Looking back," he writes, "for the first time in my life I began to see that, if Jesus Christ were really the Person He claimed to be, then He had the answers to my problems as a student body president, as well as to those in my own personal life." Presently, he is devoting his full time to introducing others to Christ through the student Christian movement of Campus Crusade for Christ International.

Recently, Dr. James Engel, a professor of marketing at Ohio State University, made this statement: "I have had enough of the garbage we hear so much about on the college campus today, that Christianity is for misfits—for the intellectual slob who can't stand on his own two feet and face the world. There are thousands of men and women on college and university faculties today who, like myself, are just plain fed up with this kind of attack on our intelligence and the validity of our faith.

"Jesus Christ has changed our lives completely, and we're not about to be silenced by a bunch of ill-informed critics who refuse to face the facts about the greatest Person who ever lived. We're not about to sit back while the 'anti-God squad' rules the campus. This is serious business. Make no mistake about it—what you believe about Christ is a life or death matter. Kick Christ in the face if you want, but be prepared to pay the price. I don't know about you, but to me the prospect of life forever without God just doesn't make sense when He offers us so much."

Phil Johnson from California State College, Long Beach, California, says, " 'For me to live is Christ.'

"This is a verse that I have found very true and relevant in my life. Like many other Christians today, I was a very active church member before I came into a personal relationship with Christ. Now I challenge people of all races to find Christ as their personal Savior.

"As a Negro, and as an athlete, I find many problems that cannot be solved without Christ. There is no hope for mankind through rioting, drugs, parties and sex. For Christ said, 'I am come that they might have life and that they might have it more abundantly.' "[2]

Wayne Collier, from the University of Oregon, shares, "It has been five years since I invited Jesus Christ into my life, and to be honest, it hasn't all been stable fellowship. But I have found that the problems arise when I try to live the Christian life according to what I think it should be—convicting and condemning myself for little things.

"But actually, I have been free since I first opened my heart to Christ, for He died for all of my sins 2,000 years ago. I am learning to just thank Him and love Him. I realize now that I can accept myself just the way I am because that's how God loves me. Now I am free to love anyone and everyone unconditionally, regardless of whether they love me in return. It is tremendous to have a friend like Jesus, for He enables me to live an abundant life."

Linda Fulcher, sophomore at the University of Oregon, describes her relationship with Christ: "For a long time I sat in church and never really believed all that I was hearing. Finally I came to the place where I had to either take Christ completely at His word or reject Christianity in its entirety. My decision to completely trust Christ, not only with my whole life, but also by daily turning over to Him everything about my life—friends, studies, dates, money problems, etc.—made a total difference in the type of Christian life that I then began to live.

"I especially noticed a change in my studies. I had a real purpose in studying, and I found that as I did my part and then just trusted Christ for His peace, I had won the battle. Christ has proved that He is relevant to every area of my life."

Mark Eastman, editor, *The Fortyniner*, California State, Long Beach, '68, stated in an editorial, "Beyond Human Solution:"

" 'For the first time, it seems to me that a majority of our people have come to the conclusion that many of our problems are beyond human solution.'

"This statement was made recently by California Congressman, Alphonzo Bell. Representative Bell, speaking at a Rotary Club luncheon in Los Angeles, said that he has found a 'profound and unprecedented feeling of anger, frustration, anxiety and deep helplessness' throughout the United States.

"Says Bell, 'Rampant pessimism is remarkable in its breadth and frightening in its magnitude. It exceeds in intensity any generalized public attitude that I have experienced in my career in government.'

"As an editor, I, too have sensed an increasing mood of 'rampant pessimism' among fellow staff members, student government leaders, and citizens in the community.

"In almost every area of life, there is nothing optimistic to grasp. Representative Bell is right when he says it seems that 'a majority have come to the conclusion that many of our problems are beyond human solution.'

"As we seek solutions, the only place left to look is up. The solution needed is a spiritual one—the one that Jesus Christ alone offers."

Dick Doss was president of his fraternity, co-captain of the tennis team, had a fine singing voice, and was the life of the party. He was the kind of person who could drink and hold a little more liquor than almost anybody else—and was very popular with the coeds. Yet, he hated Christians; as a matter of fact, when some of the fellows in his fraternity house invited a Campus Crusade team to speak to a meeting of the brothers, he reacted very strongly and said, "Over my dead body will they come!" A couple of the men who wanted us to come were big, husky athletes, so they responded, "All right, that's fine with us, over your dead body."

As we entered the fraternity house, there was a spirit of apprehension because he was the kind of activist against Christianity who "ate" Christians for breakfast. During the course of the meeting, we did not talk about religion or even Christianity; but we talked about the living Christ, how God personally visited this planet, and became a man in fulfillment of prophecy; how He died on the cross for our sins, was raised from the dead, and is now waiting to take His rightful place of authority on the throne of every life.

At the conclusion of the message, I asked those who wanted to know Christ personally as their Savior and Lord to meet with me. As usual, over half of the young men in the fraternity responded, and this young skeptic and antagonist against Christianity was among the first. I asked him to have lunch with me. We sat together a few days later over lunch. As we were about to order our food, I remember vividly how, with a bit of impatience, he pushed his menu aside and said, "My friends think that I am happy because I am always the life of the party, laughing and singing and living it up. But, I am probably the most miserable fellow on this campus, and I need Jesus Christ." That day he prayed to receive Christ, and his life was absolutely transformed.

That afternoon his roommate saw him reading his Bible and asked, "Did you get religion?" Dick replied, "No, I became a Christian." His roommate made fun of him. The next morning, Dick stood before his fraternity brothers, and said, "Men, you know what a Godless fellow I've been. Yesterday, I became a Christian, and I want to go on record so that you will know that I belong to Christ and that I want to live for Him."

Scores of men and women, no doubt hundreds of them, were influenced by his life; and today, this young man has not only finished his theological training at one of the leading theological seminaries and has received his doctorate in theology, but he is now a professor on the campus of one of the leading theological seminaries of the nation. Christ met him in a revolutionary encounter. Similar experiences of tens of thousands could be shared.

A New Life!

The revolutionary encounters which I have described lead to a dynamic new kind of life—a life of cleansing from past sin and guilt. This is a life with a new base of power; an ability to help change the lives of others—a life with a commitment to a cause that will help change the world as men encounter the revolutionary Christ who continues to live His revolutionary life through those who are dedicated to Him and His cause.

This can be your experience! You can literally help to change the world—but first you must allow Jesus Christ to change you if He has not already done so. If you have not yet received Christ as your Savior, you may wish to do so right now by simply receiving Him as God's gift to you. One of the most important verses in the Bible tells us, "God so greatly loved and dearly prized the world that He gave His only begotten Son that whosoever believeth in Him should not perish but have everlasting life."[3] Now, what do you do when someone offers you a gift? You receive it, of course. That is, if you want the gift. If you want to know Jesus

Christ in the way that millions of others are meeting Him, you can do so by "receiving" Him. Chapter 1, verse 12, of the Gospel of John explains that we become sons of God when we receive Christ. "But as many as received Him (Jesus), to them gave He power to become the sons of God." If the following prayer expresses the desire of your heart, pause right now and make it your very own and the Lord Jesus Christ, the Revolutionary of revolutionaries, will come into your life and change it into a life full of meaning and purpose. Here is a suggested prayer: "Lord Jesus, I receive You as my Savior; thank You for dying for my sins and for Your resurrection power to change my life. Help me to become a revolutionary disciple for You."

If you meant this prayer, Jesus Christ the risen Son of God, has come to take up His residence in your life; your sins have been forgiven; you have become a child of God; and you are now embarked upon a revolutionary adventure, the adventure for which God created you. The following chapter will explain how the great reservoir of God's love and power, and the abundance of His blessings, are constantly and continually available to you.

[1] Philippians 1:21
[2] John 10:10
[3] John 3:16, *Amplified Bible*
[4] John 1:12

Chapter 5

Revolutionary Power

We are on a twentieth-century power binge! Sleeping under the shining hoods of our new automobiles are more horses than will ever be needed or practical. Teenagers dream of duo quads and cubic-inches-plus and then go out to glean traffic violations and high insurance rates.

Actually, we are rapidly evolving from the horsepower age into the exciting thrust stage, measured in seven digit figures. A towering space vehicle rides a four-million-pound thrust of flame into the vastness of our galaxy. Power plus! But as yet, available only to a few men.

At Pentecost, fifty days following the resurrection of Jesus, there came a demonstration of a Power so infinite that it has never yet been measured. It shook buildings and empires. It turned the world upside down. It changed the course of history. It transformed lives. It raised the dead. It healed the incurables and accomplished the impossible. And that omnipotent Power, the Power of the Holy Spirit of God, is available to you to enable you to live a holy and fruitful life for Christ. Every Christian is privileged—even more important, he is commanded in God's Word—to allow the Holy Spirit to control and empower his life. Yet, tragedy of tragedies, there are multitudes of Christians who do not even know who the Holy Spirit is, or, if they do, they do not know how to appropriate His power. Consequently, they go through life without ever experiencing the abundant life which Christ promised.

Jesus said, "I am come that they [you and I and all Christians] might have life, and that they might have it more abundantly."[1] Yet, many professing Christians are saying, "There is certainly nothing abundant about my life. I try to witness, but no one is interested in what I have to say. I experience nothing but doubts, fears, frustrations and defeat. Surely there must be something more to this Christian life, but I have never found it."

In my own experience, there was a time in my Christian ministry when I challenged Christians to witness and live holy lives for Christ, but the results were so discouraging that I began to devote most of my time and energies to speaking with non-Christians where God blessed with much more apparent results. However, as the years have passed, the Holy Spirit has helped me to see the great potential power in lukewarm Christians, if only they are awakened and harnessed for Christ. I am convinced that the lukewarm, carnal Christian can be changed into a vital, dynamic, witnessing Christian if he will surrender his will to Christ and be filled with the Holy Spirit. Again and again I am reminded of the great contrast between the church of Jesus Christ today and His church of the first century.

In J. B. Phillips' introduction to *Letters to Young Churches,* he states:

"The great difference between present-day Christianity and that of which we read in these letters (New Testament Epistles) is that to us it is primarily a performance; to them, it was a real experience. We are apt to reduce the Christian religion to a code or, at best, a rule of heart and life. To these men it is quite plainly the invasion of their lives by a new quality of life altogether. They do not hesitate to describe this as Christ living in them."

The Incredible Promise

The normal Christian life is a life of great adventure. It is a life of purpose, a life of power. Christ has given the almost unbelievable promise, "The works that I do shall you do also, and greater works than these shall you do; because I go unto my Father . . . If ye shall ask anything in my name, I will do it."[2]

While in seminary, I used to discuss this verse with other seminarians. But, we were not able to understand the meaning of it. Think of it. As Christians, we are promised that Christ will do in us and through us greater things than He did while here on earth. Now, I have at least some idea of the meaning of that promise.

Obviously, we cannot, in our own energy, accomplish what He has promised. But it is He, Himself, in all of His resurrection power living within us who will do it. As He walks around in our bodies, thinks with our minds, loves with our hearts, and speaks with our lips, He will fulfill that promise through us. The Son of man, who came to seek and to save the lost, will seek and save the lost through us.

The True Evidence

Jesus tells us, "Follow me and I will make you fishers of men."[3] He tells us in the Gospel of John, Chapter 15, verse 8, that the way we prove we are His followers is by bearing much fruit. In this way we bring great glory to God. We do not prove that we are following Jesus Christ by living good lives, by being moral, by being religious, by being active in the church, by saying our prayers or by reading our Bibles regularly. According to Jesus, we prove that we are His disciples when we bear much fruit. And here He is speaking about souls.

The fruit of the Spirit, as described in Galatians 5:22,23, is love, joy, peace, etc., but here in John, He is speaking of souls. You and I have the unspeakable privilege of introducing men and women to Jesus Christ. Every Christian has the God-given equipment to be fruitful for the Savior. From the moment we become Christians we receive the love, the power of the Spirit, the wisdom, all that we need, no matter how introverted or inadequate we may feel, to be fruitful.

We do not produce fruit apart from Christ's strength any more than the branch produces fruit apart from the vine. It is the lifegiving sap that flows up from the roots through the vine, the overflow of the vine's life, that produces the fruit.

So it is in the life of the believer. It is the Holy Spirit working through the vine, which is Jesus Christ, overflowing into the branches, the Christians, producing the fruit. I have never led anyone to Christ in my life. I never shall. There is nothing of which I can boast. I have been an instrument through whom the Spirit of God has drawn thousands to Himself, but He has done it. It is the availability that He uses. It is the faith that He honors. It is the obedience that He blesses. It is the Spirit of the Living God who does the work through us.

The Divine Command

The Scriptures command us to be filled with the Spirit. "Be not drunk with wine, wherein is excess; but be filled with the Spirit."[4] In the Greek language in which the New Testament was originally written, this verse means, "be ye being controlled, and empowered by the Spirit." And this is not just a once and for all dramatic, ecstatic moment. From the time we awaken in the morning until we go to bed at night we, as children of the living God, are commanded to be controlled by the Spirit. And it is not something that is limited just to a few people who are Christian leaders. It is not just for the evangelists, the pastors, and the teachers, but for all Christians.

In the Gospel of John, Chapter 7, we find our Savior standing before the crowd and saying, "If any man thirst, let him come unto Me, and drink. He that believeth on Me, . . . out of his innermost being shall flow rivers of living water."[5]

Do you thirst? Are you hungry for God? Do you desire to be a man, a woman, of God? Are you desirous of doing His will?

Again in the Gospel of John, Chapter 16, we see our Savior, meeting with the disciples in the upper room in His final hours upon this earth before the crucifixion. He is sharing with them truths that have filled their hearts with sorrow. He has told them of some of the events that are about to transpire. "Because I have said these things unto you, sorrow hath filled your hearts. Nevertheless I tell you the truth; It is expedient for you that I go away: for if I go not away, the Comforter will not come unto you; but if I depart, I will send Him unto you. And when He is come, He will reprove the world of sin, and of righteousness, and of judgment: . . . I have yet many things to say unto you, but you cannot bear them now. Howbeit when He, the Spirit of truth comes, He will guide you into all truth: for He shall not speak of Himself; but whatsoever He shall hear, that shall He speak; and He will show you things to come. He shall glorify Me: for He shall receive of Mine, and shall show it unto you. All things that the Father hath are Mine: therefore said I, that He shall take of Mine, and shall show it unto you."[6]

Within hours after this word to the disciples, our Lord, in fulfillment of prophecy, paid the supreme price on the cross for our sins. Forty days later He met with the disciples for the final moment of His time on this earth in His resurrection body. We read from the first chapter of the book of Acts, that Jesus "showed Himself alive after His passion by many infallible proofs, being seen of them forty days, and speaking of the things pertaining to the kingdom of God: and, being assembled together with them, commanded them that they should not depart from Jerusalem, but wait for the promise of the Father, which, He said, you have heard from Me. For John truly baptized with water; but you shall be baptized with the Holy Spirit not many days from now. When they therefore were come together, they asked of Him, saying, Lord, will you at this time restore again the kingdom to Israel? And He said unto them, It is not for you to know the times or the seasons, which the Father has put in His own power. But you shall receive power, after that the Holy Spirit is come upon you: and you shall be witnesses unto Me both in Jerusalem, and in all Judea, and in Samaria, and unto the uttermost part of the earth. And when He had spoken these things, while they beheld, He was taken up; and a cloud received Him out of their sight."'[1]

Christ had commissioned the disciples to go into all the world and preach the gospel but He said, "Don't go, until you are endued with power from on high." It is not enough that they had been with Jesus for three years or more. It was not enough that they had heard Him teach as no one had ever taught. It was not enough that they had seen Him restore sight to the blind, heal the sick, and raise the dead, not enough that He had demonstrated that He was truly the Messiah, the promised one of God. He said to them, "You must wait for something else to happen to you, you must wait until you are endued with the power of the Holy Spirit."

One should not assume any task, nor do anything in the name of Christ, unless he knows that he is filled with the Holy Spirit. And one can know that. It is not presumptuous at all. At the moment that you receive

Christ, you become a child of God; your sins are forgiven; you are filled with the Holy Spirit; and you are baptized into the body of Christ by the Spirit. At that moment you are given all of the power, love, wisdom and grace that you will ever need in order to be and to do all that God has called you to be and to do. As we shall see, if you know there is no sin in your life unconfessed, and that you have met God's conditions, then you can be assured that you are filled with the Spirit, by faith.

The Tragic Ignorance

From the moment of our spiritual birth, we have the power to go on growing toward maturity in Christ by faith. "The just shall live by faith." Yet, the average Christian, not understanding this great concept of faith, finds himself on a spiritual roller coaster, up and down, up and down, living from emotional experience to emotional experience. He becomes a carnal Christian.

In Romans 7, Paul describes the conduct of the Christian who is carnal. He says, "The good that I would I do not: but the evil which I would not, that I do . . . wretched man that I am! who shall deliver me from the body of this death?"[8]

The carnal man is a miserable man. As a matter of fact, the carnal man is far more miserable than the nonbeliever. Because, having been given a taste of the glory of God, he goes back to live the old life and yet can never be satisfied again with it.

The man who has tasted of God's love and God's forgiveness, who has been given a new nature and who knows the reality of the indwelling Christ, is never, never satisfied to live the old life again. But he does not know what to do about it. He does not know how to live by faith. He lives by feeling.

This is the great tragedy that is entrapping millions of Christians all over the world. They do not know how to stop being carnal Christians and how to become spiritual Christians and continue on the high plane of a vital personal fellowship with Christ. The only One who can enable them to do this, of course, is the Holy Spirit.

Who Is the Holy Spirit?

The Holy Spirit is God. He is not an "it." He is not a divine influence. He is not a fleecy white cloud. He is God with all the attributes of deity. Now if you were to ask me to define the Trinity, I cannot. No one can. One of my professors in seminary, a very brilliant scholar, was sharing with us one day in class, "The man who denies the Trinity will lose his soul. The man who tries to understand the Trinity will lose his mind." You see, we are finite. We cannot possibly comprehend God who is infinite. We simply try to illustrate God, but even this is impossible. I could say to you, "I have a body, a mind and a spirit, which one is Bill Bright?" I could say to you that there is an egg, the white, the yolk and the shell of the egg, which is the egg? Here is the sun. We cannot possibly see the sun. We see a ball of fire, but that is not really the sun. We might say that the sun itself is the Father; the ball of fire is Christ; and the warming rays of the sun are the

Holy Spirit. But none of these is adequate. They give us only a little glimpse of what God is like. There is only one God, eternally existing in three Persons. Christ revealed the Father, and the Holy Spirit enables us to know Christ.

What Is His Mission?

Why did the Holy Spirit come to this earth? He came to this earth to glorify Christ. He came to lead us into all truth. He inspired holy men of old to record the holy truths contained in the Bible. And as we read the Holy Word of God in faith we ourselves become holy. The Bible is as up-to-date as tomorrow morning's newspaper. I read passages of Scripture that I have read again and again and suddenly, at the moment I need a particular truth, it comes alive to me and I say, "I've never seen that before." Why? Because the Holy Spirit makes relevant the Word of God when I need it. It is a living Book inspired by the Holy Spirit. And the only person who can understand the Bible is one who is controlled by the Holy Spirit.

I pray and no one answers, unless I am controlled by the Spirit, because it is the Spirit who "maketh intercession for us with groanings that cannot be uttered."

I share God's love and forgiveness in Christ, and there is little response unless I am controlled by the Spirit. Jesus said, "Ye shall receive power, after that the Holy Spirit is come upon you: and ye shall be witnesses unto me."[9] We are to share with others the good news of God's love and forgiveness, demonstrated in Jesus Christ.

A friend of mine, a young minister, said, "I don't like

all this talk about the Holy Spirit. I like to talk about Jesus." I said, "I agree with you. And that is exactly what the Holy Spirit has come to do, to glorify Christ." I reminded him of the words of Jesus, "Except a man be born of the Spirit, he cannot enter the kingdom of God." And so it is impossible to even know Christ apart from the Spirit. It is impossible for us to pray, to live a holy life, to witness—there is nothing that we can do for the Lord Jesus, or that He will do through us, apart from the Holy Spirit of God.

What Happens?

What does it mean to be filled with the Spirit? It means very simply to be filled with Christ. Since the Holy Spirit came to glorify Christ, if I am filled and controlled by the Spirit, I shall be filled with Christ—I shall be abiding in Him; I shall be following Him; I shall be walking in the light as He is in the light; and the blood of Jesus Christ will cleanse and keep on cleansing me from all unrighteousness. If I am filled, controlled, empowered with the Spirit as I am admonished to be, the Lord Jesus will walk around in my body, think with my mind, love with my heart, speak with my lips, and He will continue seeking and saving the lost through me. That is the reason He came to this earth—to seek and to save the lost. And He has told us "there is none other name under heaven given among men, whereby we must be saved."[10] Jesus said, "I am the way, the truth, and the life: no man cometh unto the Father, but by me."[11]

Jesus said in Matthew, Chapter 4, verse 19, "Follow Me, and I will make you fishers of men." It is our responsibility to follow Christ, and it is His responsibility to make us fishers of men. Again, in the Gospel of John, Chapter 15, verse 8, Jesus refers to the importance of introducing others to Him, when He says, "You prove that you are following Me and will bring great glory to God when you bear much fruit." In other words, when you are controlled and empowered by the Living Christ, through the Holy Spirit, you will be actively sharing Christ with others. As a result, you will regularly introduce others to the Savior. If you are not actively sharing Christ and, as a result, introducing others to Him, it is indicative that you are not controlled by the Holy Spirit. It is that simple.

A careful study of the Scriptures will reveal that the belief that all I have to do to be a child of God is to live a good life is not true. It is not enough to live a good life. A man who is a cultist and denies the deity of Christ can live a good moral, ethical life. Outwardly, the only possible way that we can demonstrate that we are children of God, heirs of God, and disciples of Christ, is by producing fruit. And the only way we can introduce others to Christ is through the Holy Spirit's power.

Why Is the Average Christian Not Filled with the Holy Spirit?

The average Christian is not filled with the Holy Spirit because of a lack of information. I do not believe that the average carnal Christian desires to be carnal. I do not believe that the average nonbeliever would reject Christ if he understood who He is. Let us think for a moment about this. Can you conceive of an intelligent person saying "no" to Christ if he fully understood how much God loves him and how great are the benefits for time and eternity for all who trust in Christ—if he understood what happens when Christ comes to live within him? His sins are forgiven, he receives a whole new life, with true meaning and purpose, and life is no longer just an existence. But lacking this information, he continues to live in sin, rejecting God's love because he does not understand it. In like manner, experience has demonstrated that the average carnal man wants to become a spiritual man when he fully understands how to become a spiritual man and the benefits which will result.

God has a wonderful plan for your Christian life. He wants it to be replete with joy and power and fruitfulness. All this is available to you as, in faith, you ask for and receive the power of the Holy Spirit.

[1] John 10:10
[2] John 14:12,14
[3] Matthew 4:19
[4] Ephesians 5:18
[5] John 7:37
[6] John 16:6-8, 12-15
[7] Acts 1:3-9
[8] Romans 7:15, 24
[9] Acts 1:8
[10] Acts 4:12
[11] John 14:6

Chapter 6

A Revolutionary Appropriation

"Dear Tom:

"Thanks for your very generous gift of five hundred dollars. Only in eternity will you fully comprehend the significance of your gift. We were facing a desperate need and so we prayed. And then . . ."

Just another missionary letter? No, far more than just a letter. And far more desperate was the need than the letter indicated. There was no money to pay the native helpers and they threatened to quit working. There was no money to buy medicine for the dispensary, and lives were hanging in the balance. In the missionary's home the food cupboards were as bare as Old Mother Hubbard's. So the missionaries prayed and then came the cable, "Five hundred dollars cabled to your credit at Banningville Bank. Love. Tom."

Thrilled at this answer to prayer the missionary promised to pay the workmen, assured the dispensary patients that they would soon have their medicine, and told his wife to get her cookbooks out and get ready for plenty of food. He then traveled over a hundred miles to the Banningville Bank and handed Tom's cable and an empty money sack to the teller. In a few minutes he was on his way with five hundred dollars.

Faith prompted the missionary to pray. Through faith he promised wages, medicine and food. And because he trusted Tom, the missionary went to the bank and appropriated the money.

In exactly the same way—through belief, trust and appropriation—the believer receives the fullness of the Holy Spirit.

We cannot earn the right to be filled, but we are filled by faith. How did you become a Christian? You became a Christian by faith. "For by grace are you saved through faith, and that not of yourselves: it is the gift of God: not of works, lest any man should boast."[1] In Colossians, second chapter, verse 6, we are told, "As ye have therefore received Christ Jesus the Lord, so walk ye in him." You received Christ by faith, you walk by faith. Everything we receive from God from the moment of our spiritual birth until we die is by faith. Do you want to be filled with the Holy Spirit? You can be right now—right where you are at this moment. And you do not have to beg or barter with God to fill you. It is not necessary to fast and pray and plead with God as I have done in the past. I used to fast for a week at a time and cry out to God for His fullness. I listened to other people and read the biographies of great men who had done this, and I thought that this was the way to do it. And then I discovered that "the just shall live by faith." We do not earn His fullness.

Suppose I want to cash a check for a hundred dollars. Would I go to the bank and place the check for a hundred dollars on the counter, and then get down on my knees and say, "Oh Mister Teller, please cash my check?" No, I would simply go in faith, just as the missionary did, place the check on the counter, wait for it to be cashed, and then go away with the money and a "thank you." That is how we should come to God to receive the fullness of His Spirit.

Command and Promise

There are two words that are very important to remember: *command* and *promise*. In Ephesians, Chapter 5, verse 18, God *commands* us to be filled with the Holy Spirit. It is to be a way of life from the time we awake in the morning until we go to bed at night, all the days of our lives, till we go to be with Him. With that command is a *promise* found in I John, Chapter 5, verses 14 and 15, "This is the confidence that we have in Him, that, if we ask anything according to His will, He hears us; and if we know that He hears us, . . . we know that we have the petitions that we desired of Him." On the authority, then, of His command and His promise, you can be sure that, if you meet God's conditions you are filled with the Spirit.

Jesus said, "Except a grain of wheat fall into the ground and die, it abides alone, but if it dies, it brings forth much fruit."[2] Paul writes, "I beseech you therefore, brethren, by the mercies of God, that you present your bodies a living sacrifice, holy, acceptable unto God, which is your reasonable service."[3] There cannot be two masters on the throne. Ego—self—must abdicate the throne so that Christ can be on it. And so you say to Him, "Lord, I surrender my will to You to do Your will as You fill me with Your Spirit." Jesus said, "If any man come after Me, let him deny himself and take up his cross daily, and follow Me."[4] The amazing thing is that the cross of Christ is not a burden, but is an exciting adventure as He lives His life through us.

A Suggested Prayer

If you sincerely desire to experience the fullness and power of the Holy Spirit in your life, pray the following prayer: "Dear Father, I need You. I acknowledge that I have been in control of my own life. And as a result, I have sinned against You. I confess my sin and now ask Christ to take control of the throne of my life. Fill me with the Holy Spirit as You commanded me to be filled and promised in Your word that You would do if I asked in faith. I pray in the authority of the name of Jesus. As an expression of my faith, I now thank You for filling me with the Holy Spirit and taking control of my life."

When you prayed this prayer, you were, in essence, saying, "Lord, I am surrendering every area of my life to Your control–my family, my business, my profession, my time, my talents, my treasures. I want You to run my life from now on. I want You to be my Master. And by faith, on the authority of Your *command* that I be filled, and the *promise* that, if I ask anything according to Your will, You will hear me, and if You hear me, You will answer me, I receive your fullness." There is nothing more exciting in this world than the privilege of walking with God day after day, experiencing His love, His forgiveness, and being a channel of His blessing to others. There are fear and frustration and heartache and sorrow all around us. Men are looking for reality, and that reality is found only in the Lord Jesus.

You may be the most outstanding personality in your city, or you may be a nonentity as far as the community is concerned; but in the eyes of God you are someone—someone for whom He has died. If you are a Christian, God made you an heir—a joint heir—with Christ. You are now seated with Christ in the heavenlies. And you have been promised power and wisdom to help change the course of history; to help fulfill the Great Commission in our generation; to help take the claims of Christ to men everywhere, beginning in your own home and in your own community. You and I are men and women specially chosen and ordained of God to bring about a spiritual revolution. We cannot boast of this. It is not because we deserve to be chosen and ordained, but because He in His grace has done what He has done. And whatever happens, to Him be the glory.

[1] Ephesians 2:8,9
[2] John 12:24
[3] Romans 12:1
[4] Luke 9:23

Chapter 7

A Revolutionary Walk

There are four *spiritual* truths which if properly understood and believed will enable us to walk in the Spirit, to experience the abundantly revolutionary life which Jesus promised, and to bring glory to God through the fruitfulness of our lives and witness for Him. These are: (1) Be sure that you are filled with the Holy Spirit. (2) Be prepared for spiritual conflict. (3) Know your rights as a child of God. (4) Live by faith.

Be Sure that You Are Filled

First, in order to walk in the Spirit, we must be sure that we are filled with the Spirit. In Ephesians 5:18, we are admonished, "Be not drunk with wine, wherein is excess; but be filled with the Spirit." To be filled with the Spirit means to be controlled and empowered by the Spirit. We cannot have two masters. There is a throne in every life. Either self (ego) is on that throne, or Christ is on it. This concept of Christ being on the throne is so simple that even a child can understand it.

We began to teach our sons this great truth when they were very young. One evening as we were saying our prayers together, I asked our older son, "Who is on the throne of your life?" And he said, "Jesus." And I said to the younger, "Who is on the throne of your life?" and he said, "Jesus." The next morning for breakfast, their mother had prepared a special dish called egg in a bonnet. It was a delicious thick piece of French toast with a hole in the middle, and in that little hole was a beautiful poached egg. As I was enjoying my serving, I looked over to our little lad of four-and-a-half. He was not eating his egg in a bonnet. "Brad," I said, "eat your breakfast." He replied, "I don't want it." I said, "Sure you do; you'll enjoy it. Look at me; I'm enjoying it." "Well," he said, "I don't like it and I'm not going to eat it." Being a bit dramatic, he began to release a few tears. I had to make up my mind as to what to do. I could either say to him, "Now, young man, you eat that breakfast or I'll meet you in my room with my belt;" or "Forget it, I'll eat it myself—it's better than I thought it would be." However, I thought of a better idea, and said, "Brad, who is on the throne of your life this morning?" With that, the tears really began to pour. He understood the point that I was making. He had learned this concept that Christ must be on the throne; and Christ was on the throne of his life, but not at that moment. I repeated, "Who is on the throne?" And through his tears, he replied, "The devil and me." I said to him, "Whom do you want on the throne?" He answered, "Jesus." So I said, "Let's pray," and he prayed, "Dear Jesus, forgive me for being disobedient and help me to like this egg." God heard that prayer, and he enjoyed the egg; as a matter of fact, he ate it all. You see, he had said that he did not like it before he had ever tasted it. We adults are a lot like that sometimes.

That evening, as we were saying our prayers, I asked Zachary, our older son, who had been on the throne of his life that day, and he said, "Jesus." And I asked Bradley, "Who has been on the throne of your life?" He said, "Jesus." "Oh," he added, "except for breakfast." It is such a simple truth; and yet in its distilled essence, that is what the Christian life is all about—just keeping Christ on the throne. We do this when we understand how to be filled with the Spirit.

Remember two words: *command*—"Be ye being filled," that is, be constantly and continually controlled and empowered by the Spirit; and *promise*—"if we ask anything according to God's will, He hears us; and if we know that He hears us in whatever we ask, we know that we have the requests which we have asked from Him."[1] He answers us. On the authority then of God's command and God's promise, we know that we are praying according to the will of God when we ask Him to fill us, to control us.

Now remember, the Holy Spirit already dwells within the believer. You do not have to ask Him to come to you; He is already indwelling you. Your body is a temple of God from the moment you become a Christian. So you are simply saying to Him, "I surrender the will of my life to You and by faith I appropriate Your fullness."

Do not look for feelings. The very act of looking for an emotional experience is a denial of the concept of faith. The Bible says that the just shall live by faith[2] and that without faith, it is impossible to please God;[3] and that, that which is not of faith is sin.[4] You can know right now that you are filled with the Holy Spirit; and, as you continue to walk by faith, you can continue in that assurance. In order to walk in the power of the Holy Spirit, we must first take the step of being sure that we are filled.

Prepare for Attack

Second, we must be prepared for spiritual conflict if we expect to walk in the control of the Holy Spirit. You see, the Christian life is a supernatural life, and the only One who can live it is Christ. We must be prepared for battle, and we must be aware of the fact that this battle will continue as long as we live; but the battle is the Lord's. The world, the flesh, and the devil are constantly waging battle against the believer. External forces without us and internal forces within us are constantly fighting to win control over us, and we are never free from their pressure.[5] This conflict in our lives will continue as long as we live, and there will never be a time when we are free from temptation.

Though this conflict continues through life, we have nothing to fear, provided we understand who we are, who the enemy is, and how to trust the Lord to fight our battles for us. Peter tells us to let God have all of our worries, and cares, for He is always thinking about us and watching everything that concerns us. We are to be careful, watching out for attacks from Satan, our great enemy. He prowls around like a hungry lion, roaring, looking for some victim to tear apart.[6] Satan is a real foe—let there be no mistake about it.

A young minister shared with me one day, "I am afraid of Satan." I said, "You *should* be afraid of Satan, if you want to live your own life. But if you are willing to let Christ control your life, you have nothing to fear because the Bible says, 'Greater is He that is in us than he that is in the world.' Satan was defeated two thousand years ago at the cross. Though he has great power to influence man, he has only that power which he is granted of God."

This friend lives in a city where they have one of the largest zoos in the world. I said, "What do you do with lions in your city?" He replied, "We put them in a cage." I said, "Satan is in a cage. You go out to the cage in the zoo and you see a lion pacing impatiently back and forth. He is not going to hurt you. You can get right up close to the cage if you are careful and he still cannot hurt you. But stay out of that cage, or you will get into trouble! Get in the cage, and the lion will make mincemeat of you. But you have nothing to fear so long as you stay out of the cage. You have nothing to fear from Satan so long as you depend upon Christ."

The Apostle Paul warns us, "Put on all of God's armor so that you will be able to stand safe against the strategies and tricks of Satan. For we are not fighting against people made of flesh and blood, but against persons without bodies—the evil rulers of the unseen world, those mighty satanic beings and great evil princes of darkness who rule this world; and against huge numbers of wicked spirits in the spirit world."[7]

Satan and the forces of darkness are real foes. We

need to be alert to the way Satan works, but we need have no fear of him, if we are willing to trust the Lord. But if we insist upon being carnal Christians, we had better be ready for some real problems in our individual lives and in our churches.

Satan could be compared to Butch, a big neighborhood bully, who delights in beating up all the smaller children in the area. Suppose my little lad of four years of age is on his way to kindergarten, singing and swinging his little lunch pail as he dreams of building castles in the sand. Suddenly Butch steps out from his place of hiding and beats up my little lad, who returns home in tears with a bloody nose and a black eye. "Daddy, you take me to school in the future so Butch won't beat me up," he says. So, the next day I take him by the hand and we walk to school together. As we approach Butch's place of hiding, my son says, "Watch out, Daddy, he will beat us up." But several days go by and we see no further sign of Butch. After a while my son says, "Daddy, I guess Butch has moved away. Now I can go to school on my own." So, off to kindergarten he goes, when suddenly and without warning he is pounced upon by Butch, who had never left, but had been waiting every day, observing us as we walked to school together. He did not dare to attack while I was with my lad, but the moment I was no longer there to protect him, he attacked again.

So it is in our relationship with Christ—we are totally dependent upon Him. Satan will have no control over us, nor can he ever defeat us, so long as we look to Christ to fight our battles for us. As we abide in Him, and He remains at the control center of our lives, we can be assured of victory over every enemy when temptation comes.

Know Your Spiritual Rights

If we are going to walk in the Spirit, we need to know our spiritual rights as children of God. We need to know our heritage. We need to be able to draw upon the inexhaustible resources of God's love, power, forgiveness and abundant grace. We need to be able to not only experience these for ourselves, but to share the good news of them with others. And in order to understand this, Paul introduces his admonition to beware of Satan's tricks by saying, "I want to remind you that your strength must come from the Lord's mighty power within you."[8]

I do not have any strength in myself. I used to be self-sufficient–proud of what I could do on my own. Then I became a Christian and realized how totally incapable I am of living the Christian life; how weak I really am and yet how strong I am in Christ. Like Paul, "I can do all things through Him who strengthens me."[9] "God hath not given us a spirit of fear; but of power, and of love, and of a sound mind."[10] So Satan is defeated when we trust in Christ.

Christ's power is available to all, but "His power is available to help only those who believe Him. It is that same mighty power that raised Christ from the dead and seated Him in the place of honor at God's right hand in heaven, far, far above any other kings or ruler or dictator or leader. Yes, His honor is far more glorious than that of any one else either in this world or in the world to come. And God has put all things under His feet and made Him the supreme Head of the church—which is His body, filled with Himself, the Author and Giver of everything everywhere."[11] His power is the power upon which we are to draw.

Jesus commissioned the disciples to go into all the world and preach the gospel, with the promise that He would always be with them. He said, "I have been given all authority in heaven and earth. Therefore go and make disciples in all the nations . . . and then teach these disciples to obey all the commands I have given you."[12] He did not say to them, "Go into all the world, and good luck." He said, "And be sure of this—that I am with you always, even to the end of the world."[13] "I will never, *never* fail you nor forsake you."[14]

This One whom we serve is the omnipotent God! He is the One of whom it is said that He "is the exact likeness of the unseen God. He existed before God made anything at all, and, in fact, Christ Himself is the Creator who made everything in heaven and earth, the things we can see and the things we can't; the spirit world with its kings and kingdoms, its rulers and authorities: all were made by Christ for His own use and glory . . . For God wanted all of Himself to be in His Son. . . . In Him lie hidden all the mighty, untapped treasures of wisdom and knowledge. . . . Don't let others spoil your faith and joy with their philosophies, their wrong and shallow answers built on men's thoughts and ideas, instead of on what Christ has said. For in Christ there is all of God in a human body; so you have everything when you have Christ, and you are filled with God through your union with Christ. He is the highest ruler with authority over every other power."[15] If we have Him, we have everything we need. According to your day, shall strength be given. Do you need wisdom? He will give it. Do you need material possessions to supply your physical and material needs so that you can better serve Christ? They are available. He owns the cattle on a thousand hills, and I want to tell you that He answers prayer for every need.

In Romans, the sixth chapter, the apostle Paul writes of our heritage and of what happened to you when you became a Christian. "Your old evil desires were nailed to the cross with Him; that part of you that loves to sin was crushed and fatally wounded, so that your sin-loving body is no longer under sin's control, no longer needs to be a slave to sin. . . . So look upon your old sin nature as dead and unresponsive to sin, and instead be alive to God, alert to Him, through Jesus Christ our Lord. . . . Do not let any part of your bodies become tools of wickedness, to be used for sinning; but give yourselves completely to God—every part of you—for you are back from death and you want to be tools in the hands of God, to be used for His good purposes."[16] Oh, how wonderful to know that these members of our bodies—our eyes, our ears, our lips, our hands, our feet—can be used for the glory of God.

A young student said to me at an institute, "If I give my life to Christ, do I become a puppet?" No, we never become puppets. We have the right of choice—we are free moral agents. But the more we understand the love of God and the faithfulness of God and the power of God, the more we can trust Him with every detail of our lives.

Live by Faith

If we are to walk in the Spirit, we must live by faith. Oh, how sad to see sincere, dedicated Christians, who have been deceived by the wrong emphasis on emotions. We do not live by feelings. We live by faith. Feelings are the by-product of obedience. There is nothing wrong with feelings. Thank God for them. Jesus said, "He that hath My commandments, and keepeth them, he it is that loveth Me: and he that loveth Me shall be loved of My Father, and I will love him, *and will manifest Myself to him.*"[17] Do not be ashamed of feelings, but do not look for them. Never emphasize them. Let them find their proper place in your relationship with Christ. You live according to God's promise, according to the integrity of God Himself. You see, faith must have an object. And the object of our faith as Christians is God and His Word. God has proven Himself to be worthy of our trust. There are thousands of promises, and no Christian has ever found any of them to be untrue. When He says something, you can stake your life on it—you can know that He will not fail you.

Two very important verses demonstrate the significance of faith. Paul wrote, "All things work together for good to them that love God, to them who are the called according to His purpose."[18] Do you believe that? It is a promise. Then, we are told, "In every thing give thanks; for this is the will of God in Christ Jesus concerning you."[19]

Do you give thanks when all things go wrong? Have you learned to say "thank You" when you lose a loved one? When you have financial reverses? When you fail an exam?

You may say that only a fool would do such a thing. No, not if all things work together for good to those who love God, to those who are called according to His purpose. If He has commanded us to give thanks, there is a reason for it. And let me tell you, as one who has had some experiences in this regard, that this is one of the most exciting and profitable lessons I have ever learned—the lesson of saying "thank You" when things go wrong. In previous years, I used to lose my patience when things went wrong. I made doors open. If they did not open before me, I broke them down. And then I discovered what a fool I was. I became tense inside, and was often impatient with people, and if anyone got in my way, someone had to move. Oh how tragically we can mutilate our brothers with such thoughtlessness. Christians are oftentimes this way. But God has given us a better plan. We can relax. We can say "thank You" when the whole world is crumbling around us. Why? Because the God whom we serve is sovereign and omnipotent. He holds the world in His hands. Even the hairs of our heads are numbered. We can trust Him. He loves us. He died for us. He personally visited this planet, took upon Himself our sins, and He is waiting to bless us. But He cannot bless us if we are worried. He cannot bless us if we complain and criticize and find fault.

Some time ago, a young woman came to our headquarters for one of our training institutes and she asked if she could share a problem with me. After one of my lectures, we talked together, and she shared through her tears that her heart was broken—she had lost her dearest friend, who had been killed in an accident. She had been driving the car when he was killed. They were coming home from their engagement party, and an oncoming automobile crossed the center, forcing her off the road into a telephone pole. The sadness of it, the tragedy of it, and the loss of her dearest friend were compounded by the guilt of knowing that she had been driving the car. She asked, "What shall I do?" Many months had passed, and she had gone to psychiatrists and psychologists and ministers and many other people, seeking counsel. She said, "If I find no help, I fear for my sanity." I asked, "Are you a Christian?" She said, "Yes." We read Romans 8:28 and I asked, "Do you believe this?" She said, "Yes, I believe that." We turned to I Thessalonians 5:18. I said, "Read this." She read it aloud. "In every thing give thanks for this is the will of God in Christ Jesus concerning you." I said, "Have you thanked God yet for this accident?" She looked at me with surprise and an expression of horror. "How can I ever thank God for this?" she said. I replied, "You do not trust God, do you?" "Yes, I trust God." "Then why not show that you do?" I asked. "Will you pray and tell God that you trust Him and give thanks in everything?" As we knelt together, she prayed, "God I don't understand, but I know I can trust You; and I do say 'thank You'." Now, what was she saying when she said "thank you?" She was saying to God, "I trust You." And the Bible says that without faith (trust) you cannot please God. If you complain, if you are finding fault with others, you are not trusting God. You may hate God because you have lost a loved one, or your inheritance, or a lot of money, or your business, or your health, and you say, "Why did God do this to me?" God says, "In everything, give thanks."

That young lady came to my office early the next morning literally bubbling over with joy. She said, "Last night I slept without medication for the first time since the accident. And this morning when I awakened, my heart was filled with praise and thanksgiving to God. I just cannot understand it, but I know it has something to do with what you taught me about saying 'thank You' to God."

Recently, a telephone call informed me that one of my dearest, most beloved friends had gone home to be with the Lord. I fell to my knees and said, "Oh no, it's impossible—it can't be—so much alive—so virile—so dynamic—and now, dead." And then I said, "Thank You, Lord, thank You." Immediately my heart was flooded with peace that has never left me.

There was a time when we had a particular need for over half a million dollars for our headquarters operation. Indeed the whole of a great, worldwide ministry was at stake. Because of a technicality, the rug had been pulled out from under us and we were flat on our faces. The whole work was in danger of being destroyed, and my own reputation would be shattered. When the word came to me from a friend that the money which we had been promised was no longer available, I got down on my knees in my office and said, "Lord, thank You, thank You, thank You." I shall never forget that experience, as the tears flowed down my cheeks. Everything had been sabotaged—my world had crumbled. Yet God was not dead. God can be trusted. Another day would come, and another plan far more wonderful than the first would be revealed. And before I left my knees, God gave me that assurance. Within a few weeks a better plan was developed and God demonstrated that, when we trust Him, He is faithful.

One of the greatest privileges of life is to trust God. Learn how to walk by faith. What a great opportunity is ours to walk with the King, every day of our lives, from the time we awaken in the morning until we go to bed at night.

For many years it has been my practice to begin my day the night before by reading God's Word. I like to meditate upon the Lord before I go to sleep at night. Then throughout the nightwatches, when my subconscious mind takes over, I continue to think about Him. Thus when I awaken in the morning, my first thoughts are of Him. I usually awaken with a psalm of praise on my lips, with an attitude of thanksgiving—"Oh, Lord, I thank You that I belong to You. I thank You that You live within me. And I thank You that You have forgiven my sins. I thank You that I am a child of God. Now, as I begin this day, as I continue throughout the day, I thank You that You will walk around in my body. I thank You that You will love with my heart and speak with my lips and think with my mind. I thank You that during the course of the day, You have promised to do the things through me that are greater than You did when You were here on the earth. By faith I acknowledge Your greatness, Your power, Your authority in my life. And I invite You to do anything You wish." Then I slip out of bed to my knees as a formal act of acknowledging His Lordship. Next I usually go out to run a mile or more to begin the day —because our physical bodies need to be strong, too, you know. Begin the day right—spiritually, physically, every way—walking in the fullness of His power. Oh what an adventure awaits those who trust in Him, who walk moment by moment, day by day, in the fullness and power of His Spirit.

In summary, if you desire to walk in the fullness of God's spirit, you must: first, be sure that you are filled—filled by faith—obeying the *command* to be filled and claiming the *promise* that, if we ask according to His will, He will hear and answer. Second, be ready for conflict. The enemy is a real enemy. The world, the flesh and the devil will assail. Third, know your rights as a child of God. Our strength must come from the Lord. We must abide in Him. And finally, live by faith, drawing daily upon His strength, His wisdom, His power.

[1] John 5:14, 15, NAS
[2] Galatians 3:11
[3] Hebrews 11:6
[4] Romans 14:23
[5] Galatians 5:16, 17, *LNT*
[6] I Peter 5:7-9, *LNT*
[7] Ephesians 6:11,12, *LNT*
[8] Ephesians 6:10, *LNT*
[9] Philippians 4:13, NAS
[10] II Timothy 1:7, NAS
[11] Ephesians 1:19-23, *LNT*
[12] Matthew 28:18-20, *LNT*
[13] Matthew 28:20, *LNT*
[14] Hebrews 13:5, *LNT*
[15] Colossians 1:15,16,19; 2:3,8,10, *LNT*
[16] Romans 6:6, 11,13, *LNT*
[17] John 14:21
[18] Romans 8.28
[19] I Thessalonians 5:18

Chapter 8

A Revolutionary Cleansing

The student chairman of the religious emphasis week, a sharp fraternity man on the campus where I was speaking, approached me following my message. "I must talk with you," he said. "I am afraid that I will crack up unless some one can help me." I listened as he poured out a sordid story of a life of immorality, drunkenness and deceit. He assured me that he was a Christian, that he had once enjoyed a vital, fruitful relationship with our Savior. But all of this had changed as he had become "one of the boys." Like the rest of his drinking buddies, he had become immoral and one sin had led to another while guilt piled upon guilt—"I have talked to ministers and priests and psychologists, but no one can help me," he sobbed. As he shared his heartbreak and guilt, I was asking God for wisdom in order to counsel him wisely—"What can I tell him, Lord, that others have not already told him?" Suddenly a verse flashed into my mind. I opened my Bible to I John 1:9 and asked him to read, "If we confess our sins, He is faithful and just to forgive us our sins and to cleanse us from all unrighteousness." Immediately his face lighted up, "This was once one of my favorite verses," he said. "I used to share this promise with new Christians. How do you explain that I had forgotten this wonderful promise? I do want to confess my sins; I do want Christ to take control of my life again." Following this prayer of confession he went on his way rejoicing.

A prominent citizen came to share his joy of discovery after hearing my message on God's love, forgiveness and cleansing as explained in this chapter. "I could have saved myself thousands of dollars paid to psychiatrists and psychologists if only I had heard this message several years ago."

Christians do not enjoy living in defeat and frustration. But most Christians do not know what to do about their sin. Thus they are continually plagued with guilt. Many of them have tried all kinds of moral detergents but to no avail. Resolutions, reforms, social adjustment, therapeutic psychology—all of these have failed to produce a "new creation." The only hope is a revolutionary cleansing, and the only agent able to accomplish this is the blood of Jesus Christ. "If we walk in the light, as He (God) is in the light, we have fellowship one with another, and the blood of Jesus Christ, His Son, cleanses us from all sin."[1]

A Life of Adventure

The Christian life is a life of adventure. God never planned the Christian life to be an experience of constant defeat and defilement. Jesus came that we might have life—abundant, clean, victorious life.[2]

Every day can be void of guilt complex and filled with meaning, purpose, joy, victory and power when we walk in the fullness of the Holy Spirit. This cleansed life can be maintained only by God's power, not our will power. The living Christ within makes all the difference between victory and defeat.

In his preface to *The Young Church in Action,* J. B. Phillips writes, "No one can read this book (Acts) without being convinced that there is Someone at work here besides mere human beings. Perhaps because of their very simplicity, perhaps because of their readiness to believe, to obey, to give, to suffer, and if need be to die, the Spirit of God found what surely He must always be seeking—a fellowship of men and women so united in love and faith that He can work in them and through them with a minimum of hindrance."

The first-century church was able to make such an impact for God because it was composed of spiritual Christians—men and women filled with, cleansed by and completely controlled by the Holy Spirit.

The Word of God tells us that there are three kinds of people in the world: the natural, the carnal and the spiritual.[3]

The natural man is not a Christian. He depends upon his own resources and lives in his own strength. He cannot understand or accept the divine truths of God's Word. His interests and ambitions are centered in things fleshly and worldly.

When a man receives Christ as his Savior and Lord he becomes a spiritual man. Jesus said, "You must be born of the Spirit." At the moment of spiritual birth the Christian is filled with the Holy Spirit, through whose power this relationship with God is made possible. At the same time he is also cleansed of all sin, becomes a child of God and experiences the joy of his salvation. However, for most Christians the walk in the control of the Holy Spirit is short-lived. The radiance, joy and contagious enthusiasm of knowing Christ personally is soon gone and the Christian begins to try to serve God in the energy of the flesh instead of living by faith. The Bible says, "The just shall live by faith."[4] "And without faith it is impossible to please God. . . ."[5] ". . . that which is not of faith is sin."[6] The experience of trying to please God by our good works—through self or fleshly effort instead of trusting Christ to enable us to live a supernatural life by His indwelling Holy Spirit—leads to carnality.

The Carnal Christian

The carnal man is described by Paul in I Corinthians, "And I, brethren, could not speak unto you as unto spiritual, but as unto carnal, even as unto babes in Christ. I have fed you with milk, and not with meat: for hitherto ye were not able to bear it, neither yet now are ye able. For ye are yet carnal: for whereas there is among you envying, and strife, and divisions, are ye not carnal, and walk as men?"[7]

Most Christians are carnal whether or not they realize it. One man said, "I didn't know I was carnal. I have heard my pastor talk about carnal Christians many times but I always thought he meant somebody else. Now I realize that I, too, am carnal."

Paul tells us more about this type of Christian, when he writes, "The law is good, then, and the trouble is not there but with me, because I am sold into slavery with sin as my owner. I don't understand myself at all, for I really want to do what is right, but I can't. I do what I don't want to—what I hate. I know perfectly well that what I am doing is wrong, and my bad conscience proves that I agree with these laws I am breaking. But I can't help myself because I'm not doing it. It is sin inside me that is stronger than I am that makes me do these evil things. I know I am rotten through and through so far as my old sinful nature is concerned. No matter which way I turn I can't make myself do right. I want to but I can't. When I want to do good, I don't; and when I try not to do wrong, I do it anyway."[8]

Some time ago I was passing through a certain community and while there called a friend I have known for many years. He is an outstanding Christian businessman, who has prayer and Bible study daily with his employees, and is a Christian leader in his community. Instead of greeting me with his usual, "It's great to be a Christian," he answered my phone call with the words, "I wish the Lord would take me home." He agreed to come to see me, and as we talked he said, "I am a hypocrite. I tell people how wonderful it is to be a Christian. But it isn't wonderful. I am miserable. I was happier before I became a Christian."

He went on to tell me about all the things that he had done in an attempt to please God. Some of his Christian friends had told him that he needed to work hard at being a Christian and that he should be praying more and memorizing Bible verses. Other friends said to him, "You are working too hard at this thing. Just let go and let God control your life." He said to me, "Between hanging on and letting go, I've had a rough time of it." Here was one of the most sincerely motivated men I have ever known but he was a carnal Christian, trying to live for God in the energy of the flesh.

Paul continues his description of the carnal Christian, "Now if I am doing what I don't want to, it is plain where the trouble is; sin still has me in its evil grasp. It seems to be a fact of life that when I want to do what is right, I inevitably do what is wrong. I love to do God's will so far as my new nature is concerned; but there is something else deep within me, in my lower nature, that is at war with my mind and wins the fight and makes me a slave to the sin that is still within me. In my mind I want to be God's willing servant but instead I find myself still enslaved to sin. So you see how it is: my new life tells me to do right, but the old nature that is still inside me loves to sin. Oh, what a terrible predicament I am in! Who will free me from my slavery to this deadly lower nature? Thank God! It has been done by Jesus Christ our Lord. He has set me free."[9]

Upon reading this, one of my friends said, "That is my biography—the story of my life."

The Great Discovery

Every Christian has this same problem until he makes the discovery that Paul made: "Thank God! It has been done through Jesus Christ our Lord. He has set me free. So there is now no condemnation awaiting those who belong to Christ Jesus. For the power of the lifegiving Spirit—and this power is mine through Christ Jesus—has freed me from the vicious circle of sin and death. We aren't saved from sin's grasp by knowing the commandments of God, because we can't and don't keep them, but God put into effect a different plan to save us. He sent His own Son in a human body like ours—except that ours are sinful—and destroyed sin's control over us by giving Himself as a sacrifice for our sins."[10]

How well I remember the years of seeking after God with all my heart. I resorted to all kinds of self-imposed disciplines, begging God for His power. The more I tried, the more defeated and frustrated I became. Then the great realization dawned on me, as I read, "The old sinful nature within us is against God. It never did obey God's laws and it never will."[11] What a relief it was to me to discover that I would never be able to live the Christian life through my own efforts. But I could trust Christ to live His resurrection life in and through me. It is faith, not self-effort; trusting, not trying, that pleases Him.

What is faith? Faith is another word for trust. Faith must have an object and the object of the Christian's faith is God and His Word. God's Word tells us that we need not continue to be defeated, carnal, fruitless and impotent Christians. We can be revolutionaries for God, and that is what He has called us to be. Jesus gave us the incredible but reliable promise that if we believe on Him we will be able to do greater works than He did. He assured us that whatsoever we would ask in His name, He will do it.[12] No Christian need continue this life as a carnal man. Christ has both the power and the willingness to deliver us from carnality.

It is tragically true that the average Christian is a practical atheist. He professes to believe in God, yet he acts as though God either does not exist or is unwilling to deliver him. With all the resources of God available, he lives in self-imposed spiritual poverty. He fails to act like a child of the King, or to live like one who is adopted into royalty from a state of poverty and illiteracy. How can the carnal man get off and stay off this emotional plane and overcome his up-and-down, spiritual roller coaster type of existence?

A Revolutionary Concept

One of the greatest spiritual concepts which I have ever learned and one which has been used to change the lives of multitudes of Christians is a concept which I like to call "Spiritual Breathing." Just as we exhale impure air and inhale pure air physically, so, in spiritual breathing, we exhale when through faith in God's promise we confess our sins, and we inhale when we appropriate the fullness of God's Spirit by faith.

As I confess, I acknowledge that ego, self, is on the throne of my life. I recognize a particular sin and realizing the wrong of this sin, I confess it. The word "confess" means "say along with" or "agree with." Thus, when I confess my sins, I am agreeing with God concerning my sins. In other words, I am telling God that I love Him and desire to please Him more than I love my sin. Further, since God promised that my sins were forgiven at the cross, by faith I accept the fact that I am forgiven and cleansed. I receive His forgiveness and cleansing by faith. By faith I turn from what I have been doing wrong, and do what God wants me to do. This is repentance in the truest sense of the word. In agreeing with God concerning my sin, I demonstrate a change of attitude and this change of attitude results in a change in my conduct.

What is the basis for our forgiveness? It is Christ's death on the cross, as the substitute for our sin. The tenth chapter of Hebrews beautifully explains God's gracious provision for our sins. "The old system of Jewish laws gave only a dim foretaste of the good things Christ would do for us. The sacrifices under the old system were repeated again and again, year after year, but even so they could never save those who lived under their rules. If they could have, one offering would have been enough; the worshipers would have been cleansed once for all, and their feelings of guilt would be gone. But just the opposite happened: those yearly sacrifices reminded them of their disobedience and guilt instead of relieving their minds. For it is not possible for the blood of bulls and goats to really take away sins. That is why Christ said, as He came into the world, 'O God, the blood of bulls and goats cannot satisfy You, so You have made ready this body of Mine for Me to lay as a sacrifice upon Your altar. You were not satisfied with the animal sacrifices, slain and burnt before You as offerings for sin.' Then I said, 'See I have come to do Your will, to lay down My life, just as the Scriptures said that I would.' After Christ said this, about not being satisfied with the various sacrifices and offerings required under the old system, He then added 'Here I am. I have come to give My life.' He cancels the first system in favor of a far better one. Under this new plan we have been forgiven and made clean by Christ's dying for us once and for all. Under the old agreement the priests stood before the altar day after day offering sacrifices that could never take away our sins. But Christ gave Himself to God for our sins as one sacrifice for all time, and then sat down in the place of highest honor at God's right hand, waiting for His enemies to be laid under His feet. For by that one offering He made forever perfect in the sight of God all those whom He is making holy. And the Holy Spirit testifies that this is so, for He has said, 'This is the agreement I will make with the people of Israel, though they broke their first agreement: I will write My laws into their minds so that they will always know My will, and I will put My laws in their hearts so that they will want to obey them.' And then He adds, 'I will never again remember their sins and lawless deeds.' Now, when sins have once been forever forgiven and forgotten, there is no need to offer more sacrifices to get rid of them."[13]

Paul writes to the Church in Rome, "But God shows and clearly proves His [own] love for us by the fact that while we were still sinners Christ, the Messiah, the Anointed One, died for us. Therefore, since we are now justified—acquitted, made righteous and brought into right relationship with God—by Christ's blood, how much more [certain it is that] we shall be saved by Him from the indignation and wrath of God. For if while we were enemies we were reconciled to God through the death of His Son, it is much more [certain], now that we are reconciled, that we shall be saved [daily delivered from sin's dominion] through His [resurrection] life."[14]

If you are a Christian, your sins have been forgiven. You cannot add one iota to what Christ has already done for you upon the cross. Tears, good works, self-efforts and penances cannot provide reconciliation to God. They are not needed. It is faith that makes what Jesus Christ has already done for us a reality in our personal experience. Faith motivates us to repent and repentance leads us to turn from what we have been doing to doing what God wants us to do.

In Hebrews we discover that what man tried to do concerning his sins, Christ did for him by His death on the cross and by shedding His blood. We cannot add anything to what Christ has done. We simply accept His forgiveness and cleansing by faith.

You may say, "If Christ has already paid the penalty for my sins—past, present and future—once and for all, I might as well live it up and have a ball sinning." John deals with this attitude as, immediately after explaining confession and cleansing, he writes, "My little children. I am telling you this so that you will stay away from sin. But if you sin, there is Someone to plead for you before the Father. His name is Jesus Christ, the One who is all that is good and who pleases God completely. He is the One who took God's wrath against our sins upon Himself, and brought us into fellowship with God; and He is the forgiveness for our sins, and not only ours but all the world's. And how can we be sure that we belong to Him? By looking within ourselves! Are we really trying to do what He wants us to?"[15] The man who treats sin casually is not likely to be a Christian, according to God's Word.

The Importance of Confession

A further question may come to your mind, "If Christ has paid the penalty for my sins, as a Christian why do I have to confess?" Confession is agreeing with God concerning your sins and is necessary for the simple reason that it makes a reality in your experience of the forgiveness and cleansing which Christ has provided for you at the cross. If you refuse to confess your sins, you become carnal and walk in the shadows instead of walking in the light. For example, in the thirty-second Psalm, David explained, "When I kept silence (when he did not confess his sins), my bones waxed old through the roaring all the day long. For day and night Thy hand was heavy upon me: my moisture is turned into the drought of summer. . . . I acknowledged my sin unto Thee and mine iniquity have I not hid. I said, I will confess my transgressions unto the Lord; and Thou forgavest the iniquity of my sin. . . . Restore unto me the joy of Thy salvation; and uphold me with Thy free spirit. Then will I teach transgressors Thy ways; and sinners shall be converted unto Thee."[16] The loving chastisement of the Lord will inevitably result when we fail to confess our sins. There is another good reason for confession of sins, and that is to avoid the chastening of the Lord. Chastening should not be confused with wrath or punishment. The Bible says ". . . those whom the Lord loves He disciplines, and He scourges every son whom He receives. It is for discipline that you endure; God deals with you as with sons; for what son is there whom his father does not discipline?

"But if you are without discipline, of which all have become partakers, then you are illegitimate children and not sons. Furthermore, we had earthly fathers to discipline us, and we respected them; shall we not much rather be subject to the Father of spirits, and live?

"For they disciplined us for a short time as seemed best to them, but He disciplines us for our good, that we may share His holiness. All discipline for the moment seems not to be joyful, but sorrowful; yet to those who have been trained by it, afterwards it yields the peaceful fruit of righteousness."[17]

It should be understood that God is "child-training" us, not paying us back for sins we have committed.

Furthermore, chastening is never given of God as punishment for sins. Christ's death on the cross has once and for all satisfied the wrath and justice of God for the believer's sin. Chastening or disciplining is always for the purpose of "child training"—God the Father helping His children to grow and mature spiritually. Yet, chastening can be a grievous experience or "spanking" which can be avoided by confession of our sins. According to I Corinthians 11:31,32, "If we would judge (carefully examine) ourselves we should not be judged. But when we are judged, we are chastened by the Lord, that we should not be condemned with the world."

When a believer sins, the indwelling Holy Spirit will prompt him to acknowledge his sin. The believer will know "this is wrong." At that point the believer must "judge himself," in other words confess his sin. If he does not, he will be chastened until he is willing to confess his sins. This happened to David after his sin with Bathsheba, and God's hand was heavy upon him. He became miserable. Finally he could stand this state of broken fellowship with his Heavenly Father no longer and he became honest about his sin. When he confessed, his misery was replaced with joy and freedom.

Hear David's prayer of confession, "Oh loving and kind God, have mercy. Have pity upon me and take away the awful stain of my transgressions. Oh, wash me, cleanse me from this guilt. Let me be pure again. For I admit my shameful deed—it haunts me day and night. . . . You deserve honesty from the heart; Yes, utter sincerity and truthfulness. Oh, give me this wisdom. Sprinkle me with the cleansing blood and I shall be clean again. Wash me and I shall be whiter than snow . . . Give me back my joy again. Don't keep looking at my sins—erase them from Your sight. Create in me a new, clean heart, O God, filled with clean thoughts and right desires."[18]

The Bible says, "If we are living in the light of God's presence, just as Christ does, then we have wonderful fellowship and joy with each other, and the blood of Jesus His Son cleanses us from every sin."[19]

Perhaps you have committed sins, and have not experienced God's forgiveness. You may have resentments toward other members of your family and have lost the joy of your relationship with Christ. You pray, but there is no response. You read the Bible, but get little help or joy from it. You witness for Christ, but no one responds.

God is holy and will have no fellowship with sin. Yet, God loves us even though we may have unconfessed sins in our lives. Indeed, God loves us whether we are good or bad. He loves us unconditionally, apart from our performance. On the authority of His word, He has forgiven us unconditionally because of what Christ has done for us, and we need only to confess in the true sense of the meaning of that word in order to be assured of His cleansing power. May I suggest that, as soon as you finish reading this chapter, you take a pencil and paper and make a list of every known sin in your life which the Holy Spirit calls to your remembrance, and which is hindering your walk with Christ. Then across that list, write this wonderful promise, "If we confess our sins, He is faithful and just to forgive us our sins, and to cleanse us from all unrighteousness."[20] When you have completed your list, destroy the paper on which it is written; but, before you do so, express your gratitude to the Lord that He has forgiven you through what Christ did on the cross 2,000 years ago. When we fully realize all that Christ's death on the cross means to us we shall want to praise and give thanks to Him often. Remember that faith—not tears, pleading or any other self-imposed spiritual discipline—lays hold of God's promise to forgive and cleanse us from all sin.

At a Physicians and Dentists Institute for Evangelism at Arrowhead Springs where I had spoken one evening on this subject of forgiveness, the doctors went alone to make their lists of sins which were hindering their fellowship with the Lord and their fruitfulness for Him. Early the next morning one of the doctors gave me this report: "Last night about midnight," he said, "a doctor friend of mine came to my room and told me that he had hated me for years, while pretending to be my friend. As he was making his list, God had told him that he should come and tell me and ask me to forgive him. We had the most wonderful time of prayer and God met us in a special way . . ." He added, "I wanted to tell you this in order to encourage you to keep telling people to confess their sins and to make their lists." A word of caution: do not look for sin in your life! Ask God the Holy Spirit to reveal anything which is displeasing to Him. Avoid an attitude of introspection. It is not even wise to make such a list as I have suggested except on rare occasions. If you continue to breathe spiritually, you will not find it necessary to make lists of your sins again.

God has a wonderful life for us. But He cannot bless us, He cannot use us, until we face up to this problem of sin. God is holy and righteous, eternally aflame with the glory of His perfection, and he wants us to be in our experience all that He has created us to be. His plan is that we be changed and matured into the image of His dear Son.

A young man came to me following one of my lectures, "I didn't believe I needed to make a list," he said. "I couldn't think of anything seriously wrong in my life. But as I saw others making their lists, the Spirit of God told me to do the same. Well," he concluded, "while there were no serious problems, there were a lot of little things, and the sum total of the little things had dulled the cutting edge of my life and witness for Christ."

It may be that there are no gross sins in your life, but if your heart is cold toward God; if you are lacking in faith; if you are not fruitful; there is something wrong. Tell God about it. Begin today. Let Him cleanse you with the precious blood of Christ. Then thank Him that, as He promised, your sins have been removed as far as the east is from the west—they are buried in the deepest sea. God has put them behind

His back and remembers them against you no more. Think of it! God loves us! God has forgiven us!

May I suggest that you again pause in your reading at the end of this chapter and ask the Holy Spirit to show you the sins in your life that need to be confessed; and then thank God for forgiving and cleansing you, as He promised that He would do.

You can be assured without question that today you can experience forgiveness and cleansing for all the sins of the past. Trust Christ Jesus now for a revolutionary cleansing and a victorious new life through the power of His blood and His resurrection.

Spiritual breathing, then, involves exhaling by confession; and inhaling as we appropriate the fullness of the Holy Spirit by faith, as explained in Chapter 6, "A Revolutionary Appropriation." Every Christian is commanded to be filled with the Holy Spirit as a way of life, constantly and continually controlled and empowered.[21] We have the promise of God's Word that when we ask for anything according to God's will, He hears and answers us.[22] Thus when the Holy Spirit reveals sin in your life, be quick to exhale (confess) and inhale (appropriate God's power) and keep moving for Christ. Do not tolerate sin in your life; and be satisfied with nothing less than the Spirit-filled life.

[1] I John 1:7
[2] John 10:10
[3] I Corinthians 2:14—3:5
[4] Galatians 3:11
[5] Hebrews 11:6
[6] Romans 14:23
[7] I Corinthians 3:1-3
[8] Romans 7:14-19, *LNT*
[9] Romans 7:20-25, *LNT*
[10] Romans 7:25—8:3, *LNT*
[11] Romans 8:7, *LNT*
[12] John 14:12
[13] Hebrews 10:1-18, *LNT*
[14] Romans 5:8–10, *Amplified Bible*
[15] I John 2:1–3, *Amplified Bible*
[16] Psalms 32:3-5; 51:12,13
[17] Hebrews 12:5-11, *LNT*
[18] Psalms 51:1–10, *Living Psalms*
[19] I John 1:7, *LNT*
[20] I John 1:9
[21] Ephesians 5:18
[22] I John 5:14,15

Chapter 9

A Revolutionary Love

Science cannot perform miracles. Technicians may attempt to, and they actually do accomplish the incredible, but they cannot accomplish the impossible. Only God can. And God's greatest miracle is the transformation of a life.

Intellectually brilliant, ruthlessly ambitious, fanatically religious—this was Saul of Tarsus. Utterly devoted to the annihilation of the Christian faith, he became a bloody robot of destruction. Compassion, pity, mercy—these had long since died in the soul of this Jewish zealot. Sex and age meant nothing to him. He existed only to kill and destroy.

And then, he saw a Light and he heard a Voice. For the first time there burst from his lips an expression of submission, "Lord." The master was mastered. The prosecutor was arrested. The steel was melted and the stone, shattered. The proud, ruthless persecutor became the willing bond slave of the One he had attacked. The life of violence and murder became a life of compassion and love.

What a miracle! And that one miraculously changed life set in motion a chain reaction of miracles that shook Asia and Europe.

God literally wants to perform miracles in us and through us today! The Christian life is a miraculous life. It is a supernatural life. It is not a life of doing the best we can for God. It is God doing what we allow Him to do through us as we live by faith.

An Impossible Life

The Christian life is impossible for us to live. No one can live it—the only one who can live the Christian life is the Lord Jesus. And if we live it as He has commissioned us to live it, as He has made it possible for us to live it, it will be a supernatural life. The average person does not understand this; therefore, he lives in defeat and frustration. He does not draw upon the resources of God.

Some time ago I was visiting in a west Texas community where my brother works for a major oil company. He took me out into the country to the largest pool of oil that had ever been discovered until recent years. It is known as the Yates Pool. He showed me wells that were producing many thousands of barrels of oil a day. Then he told me the story of how this property was owned by a man named Yates, a sheep rancher. He used to graze his sheep over those rolling west Texas hills. He was living in poverty, on relief. It was during the depression years and there was not enough money to buy food and clothing for the family. I am sure that, as he grazed his sheep, he often wondered where his next meal would come from. And then one day an oil company sent a seismographic crew into the area and they said, "We believe there is oil on your property and we would like to drill a wildcat test." He signed the contract and they began to drill. At a thousand and fifteen feet, they discovered oil. They did not discover a pool—they discovered an ocean of oil. The first well came in at around 80 thousand barrels of oil a day. Now oil is worth about $3.00 a barrel. When you multiply 80,000 by $3.00 you get almost a quarter of a million dollars a day. But the next well was a hundred and eighty thousand barrels, which would mean that about a half million dollars worth of oil could be produced from that one well in a single day. And then there were many wells—they were everywhere. As a matter of fact, two years ago, the government after all these years, did a test on one of the wells and discovered that it still had the potential of flowing a hundred and twenty-five thousand barrels of oil a day, and Mr. Yates owned it all. It was all his. Yet, he was living in poverty on relief. Can you imagine? He was a multi-billionaire but he was living in poverty. I do not know of a better illustration of the carnal life than this. The moment we become children of God, heirs of God, all the resources of God are made available to us.

Do You Need Wisdom?

"If any of you lack wisdom, let him ask of God, that giveth to all men liberally, and upbraideth not; and it shall be given him. But let him ask in faith, nothing wavering. For he that wavereth is like a wave of the sea driven with the wind and tossed. For let not that man think that he shall receive anything of the Lord."[1]

Do You Need Love?

Do you lack love? You receive God's love by faith. You receive His wisdom by faith, and you receive His power by faith. Everything you need to be men and women of God is available to you. But most Christians live in self-imposed spiritual poverty because they do not understand how to release the power and love and wisdom and grace of God for their own lives; nor as instruments of God for others.

God has commanded all believers in Christ to love with His supernatural love. Jesus said, "Love the Lord your God with all your heart, soul and mind." This is the first and greatest commandment. The second most important is similar: "Love your neighbor as much as you love yourself'."[2]

The pagan world of the first century was impressed with the attitudes which Christians generally demonstrated for each other: "How they love one another."

God would never have commanded us to love, and have left us to love with our own limited resources. His supernatural, *agape* love is available to us by faith. Consider first the *command* to love: "This I command you, that you love one another."[3] Then consider the *promise:* "And this is the confidence which we have before Him, that, if we ask anything according to His will, He hears us. And if we know that He hears us in whatever we ask, we know that we have the requests which we have asked from Him."[4] Again, "And all things, whatsoever ye shall ask in prayer, believing, ye shall receive."[5] Do you want to love others? You can do so simply by claiming God's command and promise —even in relation to people you may not now even like. Why not make a list of people for whom you will claim God's love by faith—then be prepared for many heart-warming experiences.*

Do You Need Trust?

Compounded with this lack of understanding of how to love by faith is a failure to understand God's trustworthiness. There are many people who are afraid of God. It is amazing, but true. There is one who loves us as much as God loves us, no one cares for us as much as He cares for us. And yet, we have been so deceived by the enemy—even as Eve was deceived when the enemy said to her, "Yea, hath God said?"—that we have been believing the enemy all through the centuries. Incredible, that we should doubt the One who cares for us more than any other and believe the enemy of our souls—but we often do. Without faith it is impossible to please God.

How would you like it if your children were to come to you and say, "Mother, Daddy, I don't love you, I don't trust you any more." Can you think of anything that would hurt you more deeply? I cannot. And yet, by our attitudes most of us say that to God. The Bible is filled with thousands of promises, and yet, most of us live like practical atheists. We live as though God does not exist, even though we give lip service to Him. He

******How to Love by Faith*** **by Bill Bright will soon be published. Write for information.**

has given us all of these promises and yet we all too often ignore them.

Afraid of God?

Afraid of God? There are those who are so afraid of God that they fear that He will rap their knuckles and punish them if they make a mistake. A young man who was one of the most outstanding Christians whom I knew in college, always faithful in Bible study and prayer meetings and always memorizing Scripture, said to me one day, "You know I've never surrendered my life to Christ, because I've been afraid of God." I could hardly believe it. Then he told me how years before he had had a premonition that, if he should commit his life fully to Christ, his parents would be killed in some tragic automobile accident. He had a mental picture of this. And he was afraid to say "yes" to God for fear his parents would lose their lives and he would be put to the test by God. Now does that sound like a loving Father? Who do you think put that idea in his mind? That was not a premonition from God. That was Satan saying, "You can't trust God."

I seldom take a trip that I do not hear a voice—not an audible voice, but just as real—saying, "You had better take a good look at your sons and your wife and tell them how much you love them. You are never going to see them again; the plane is going to crash." Ever have an experience like that? Most of you have. It is the enemy trying to confuse and frustrate. I used to listen and I was a little troubled. But now I am no longer concerned; because, even if it happens, I know that God has made provision for me and for my family. To be absent from the body is to be present with the Lord. My confidence is in Him, not in the safety of the airplane. I can trust God. He loves me and He loves you.

The Bible says the eyes of the Lord run to and fro throughout the whole earth to make Himself strong in behalf of those who love Him, whose hearts are made perfect toward Him. God cares for us.

The Love of God

The story of the prodigal son dramatically describes the love of God for man. You will remember that it is recorded in Luke, Chapter 15, that a man had two sons, and the younger told his father, "I want my share of your estate now, instead of waiting until you die." His father agreed to divide his wealth between his sons. A few days later the younger son packed all his belongings and took a trip to a distant land. There he wasted all his money on parties and prostitutes. By the time he came to his senses he was herding swine, and even their food looked good to him. So he decided to return to his father with the thought of being received as a hired hand. But when his father saw him coming, he ran to meet him, embraced and kissed him. He put the finest robe on him and gave him a ring for his finger and shoes for his feet, and held a banquet in his honor.

What a picture of God's love for us! Do you know that God loves you as much when you are bad as He does when you are good? Did you know that God's love for you is not based upon your performance for Him? He loves you unconditionally.

You may say, "How could God love me? I have been

immoral, I have lied, stolen, have even committed murder—no, God could never love me."

Do you remember the Apostle Paul? He was a murderer. Did God love and forgive him? Remember the woman caught in the act of adultery? What did Jesus say to her? "Neither do I condemn you." But, He also said something else to her, "Go and sin no more."[6]

God's Word tells us in Romans, Chapter 5, verse 8, that God proved His love for us in that while we were yet in our sins Christ died for us. Romans, Chapter 8, verses 37 to 39, reminds us that nothing can separate us from the love of God.

In John's Gospel, Chapter 17, verse 23, we find in that great recorded prayer of Jesus to the Father, He prayed, "So that the world will know you sent Me and will understand that You love them as much as You love Me."

Finally, we are reminded again of God's love in John's first epistle, Chapter 4, verses 16 to 19, "We know how much God loves us because we have felt His love and because we believe Him when He tells us that He loves us dearly. God is love, and anyone who lives in love is living with God and God is living in Him. And as we live with Christ, our love grows more perfect and complete; so we will not be ashamed and embarrassed at the day of judgment, but can face Him with confidence and joy, because He loves us and we love Him too. We need have no fear of someone who loves us perfectly; His perfect love for us eliminates all dread of what He might do to us. If we are afraid, it is for fear of what He might do to us, and shows that we are not fully convinced that He really loves us. So you see, our love for Him comes as a result of His loving us first."

Can you trust our loving God and Father with your life, now that you understand how very much He loves and cares for you?

Are you afraid of God? Weighted down with sin and guilt? Turn to Christ right now and receive His love and forgiveness. He is eager to bless and enrich your life if only you will trust Him.

No one has taught me more about the love of God than have my two sons. I remember when I went to the hospital to get our first son. He weighed nine pounds and ten ounces, and oh, how I loved him. As I held him in my arms for the first time, it was as though I were holding a piece of my own heart. And my love for that little lad has grown through the years. Then his little brother came along, and I found that I loved him as much as I loved his older brother. I like to be with them. I just like to talk to them. When I am home I like to play with them. And they know that, no matter how busy I am, they and their mother come first. They know that, even if I am meeting with a most important person, they can still come into my office unannounced. They know that they are first in my human relationships. I love them and I tell them so, so often that I have asked them, "Do you get tired of hearing Daddy tell you that he loves you?" The answer, of course, is always "No."

Everybody wants to be loved. Psychiatrists and psychologists tell us that every person needs to be loved, and needs to know how to love. That is basic in all of our human relationships.

Love Can Be Trusted

I love my two sons, and they love me. Suppose, for the sake of illustration, when I return home after a trip they greet me with these words, "Daddy, we have missed you and we have decided that we will do anything you want us to do from now on. We will shine your shoes, we will carry in wood for the fireplace, we will run errands, anything you want, you tell us and we will do it." Now if I were to respond to that attitude as many people think that God will respond to them when they say, "Lord we will do anything you want us to do," what do you think I would do? I would take them by the shoulders and shake them and say, "I have been waiting for this. I will make you regret this decision as long as you live. I am going to take all the fun out of your life. You must eat spinach three times a day." No, do you know what I would do? I would put my arms around these little guys and I would love them all the more, if that were possible. I would go out of my way to demonstrate my love for them. I am only a man, sinful and unworthy. I do not have the ability to love as God loves. God, with His inifinite love, reaches out to us and ministers to us in our deepest need. If we can trust one another, surely we can trust God. We can trust someone who cares for us as much as He cares.

A young man who had great aspirations came to me one day. He loved adventure. He had wonderful plans for his life, and he said, "If I become a Christian I am afraid God will change my plans." And I said, "Of course He will, I hope He does, because your plans are so unworthy in comparison with His plans. You have a finite mind, and God is infinite. God is the One who created you. He is the only one who knows why you are here. And as you give your life to Him, as you allow Him to control you, you'll understand why you are on this earth." I asked, "Have you ever considered how much God loves you? How great is His sacrifice for you? How great is His power in your behalf? If you have, you'll have no difficulty saying 'no' to self and 'yes' to Christ." And he said, "I see this now, I will trust Him." I remember that, as we knelt together and prayed, he said, "Lord I'll do anything You want me to do." Today this young man is being used of God in a mighty way. It would not be an exaggeration to say that thousands of people have come to Christ through his ministry. He has reached individuals who in turn are reaching thousands, because he truly met Christ and became a disciple. In his fraternity house he was the first Christian. Within eight years there were thirteen in that secular fraternity who had gone into Christian work. Since that time, there have been many more. God has continued to do great things through this one man because he trusts the Lord with his life.

Now you do not need to worry about what is going to happen to you. It may be that you are afraid that if you commit your life fully to Christ and say, "Lord, I want You to fill me with Your Spirit," He will take away your pleasures, cause you to give up your business or your estate, and send you to some remote part of the world, where you will lose your life for Him. It may well be that this will be what He will ask you to do, but not likely. If He does, you will rejoice in the privilege.

Some of the happiest people I have ever met are out

in the remote parts of the world. They are serving Christ in primitive areas; but, should you ask them if they are happy they would say, "I'm happy as I've never known happiness before." They come home on a furlough and they can hardly wait to get back to their responsibility on the field. Oh, we can trust God. If He leads you to give up anything, He will give you more than you would ever receive apart from His grace.

My wife and I used to be very materialistic and very ambitious. But one day, she went to one room and I to another in our home in the Hollywood Hills, and we signed a contract with the Lord. We made a list of all the things we had wanted out of life, all the fine expensive things that we had desired—and we had luxurious appetites—and then we said, "Lord, we want to surrender all of our own plans and desires to You. We are turning our backs upon the things that have encumbered us so that we might serve You better. You have commanded us to seek first the kingdom of God. Now we want to seek first Your kingdom. We want to serve You and do whatever You want us to do." Today, we own very little—only our clothing and a few personal items. We literally live from day to day. We do not have a savings account. This may not be what God will call you to do. I say this for His glory, I could not be as happy if I were a multimillionaire. There is nothing in this world that compares with seeking first the kingdom, keeping Christ in control, doing what He calls us to do, being an instrument through whom He wishes to change lives. This is living for real.

You have the privilege, all of us have the privilege, of helping to change the world. And there is nothing more important. This life will soon be over. We can eat only one meal at a time. We can wear but one suit or one dress at a time. We cannot take anything with us when we die, and the money we leave behind for our children—on the basis of what we see in the lives of other Christians who have left large estates to their families—is likely to curse them. So we do not expect to leave anything to our children except the example of a love for Christ, the ability to work hard, and the prayer that they will be used of God. We believe that the greatest things which we can leave them are a good example and a rich heritage in Christ.

The world is waiting to be reached, the world is waiting to hear the good news of God's love and God's forgiveness, and too many Christians are weighted down with material things. There is nothing wrong with money. And there is nothing wrong with the ability to make money. I thank God for successful businessmen who know how to make it, and who know how to invest it for His kingdom. How sad it is when men who claim to be followers of Christ hoard that which God has given them and do not allow Him to use their treasures as well as their time and talents.

Let us not forget that our treasures always become the depositories of our affections. How foolish to love the world and the things that are in it when some day it shall pass away. But if we do the will of God, we shall abide forever, and our lives will be greatly blessed and enriched in this life.

Jesus said, "He that hath My commandments, and keepeth them, he it is that loveth Me! and he that loveth Me shall be loved of My Father, and I will love him, and will manifest Myself to him."[7]

Love is the greatest power known to man according

to I Corinthians, Chapter 13. Every Christian must learn to love with God's love by faith if we are to be used of God to help change the world.

[1] James 1:5-7,
[2] Matthew 22:37-39, *LNT*
[3] John 15:17, NAS
[4] I John 5:14,15, NAS
[5] Matthew 21:22,
[6] John 8:11,
[7] John 14:21,

Chapter 10

Revolutionary Power of Prayer

Has it ever occurred to you that as you kneel in your place of prayer you have been given the privilege of being used of God to change the lives of men and nations? God has literally made available to you a vast reservoir of power, wisdom, and grace beyond words to define, if only you are willing to believe Him.

God said to Jeremiah, "Call unto Me, and I will answer thee, and show thee great and mighty things, which thou knowest not."[1]

Remember, the One who made that statement is the One who is the mighty risen Son of God in whom dwelleth all the fullness of the Godhead bodily; the One who has commissioned us to go into all the world and preach the gospel and make disciples of all the nations;[2] the One who said, "All power is given unto Me in heaven and in earth;"[3] "Lo, I am with you alway."[4] He is the One who said, "If you shall ask anything in My name, I will do it."[5]

Why then are there so few Christians whose lives are characterized by the supernatural and the miraculous? If we would take seriously these words of our Savior, and begin to claim in prayer the things that we have been promised, miracles would attend our ways; multitudes would be introduced into the kingdom; and the whole course of history would be changed. What is our position? Why is there such little evidence of the supernatural in the lives of individuals and churches and Christian organizations? No one word so describes the spirit of the Christian as does the word "unbelief." The Lord Jesus Christ has commissioned us, as a demonstration of His concern and compassion for the world, to go and share the good news of the gospel everywhere. But we huddle in unbelief in our little prayer meetings and talk of peripheral, superficial matters. We are content to see accomplished in the name of Christ that which man is capable of accomplishing through his own intellect and eloquence and organizational ability. Instead of calling upon the mighty power of God, believing God for the supernatural, we go fruitlessly on our way—impotent and unbelieving.

The Sin of Unbelief

Jesus said, "And everything you ask in prayer, believing, you shall receive."[6] It was said of our Savior, that He could do no mighty things in Nazareth because of their unbelief. Some time ago it was my privilege to visit in Nazareth, Israel, and while there I had opportunity to meet and pray with one of the outstanding citizens of this community where our Lord spent the first thirty years of His life. We were seated in the dining room of the hotel, having lunch. I had presented to him the claims of Christ, and without any encouragement from me he bowed and began to pray. As he lifted his head, having received Christ as his Savior, he said to me, "Mr. Bright, will you send someone back to Nazareth to help us share this new truth with others?" Suddenly it occurred to me that Nazareth had not changed; that very little had happened in this city because of unbelief. And I was saddened. Then as I continued to think about what is happening throughout the Christian world, I realized that this spirit of Nazareth is abroad throughout the whole of the world. God is unable to do the great and mighty things which He wants to do through us because of our unbelief. Yes, Jesus said, "Everything you ask in prayer, believing, you shall receive."

But you may ask, "How do I know when to expect God to answer my prayers? On what authority can I pray?" The Bible says that God honors faith—and another word for faith is trust. We trust our friends, and others, who have been proven worthy of our trust because of their trustworthiness—their integrity, their honesty, their dependability. The more we know them and the more they demonstrate these qualities, the more we trust them—or the more we have faith in them. In the life of the Christian, the object of our faith is God and His Word. Now the Word of God is filled with thousands of promises for the Christian. They are promises that we can believe without question. We can stake our lives on them. God does not lie to us. We need only to discover what they are by reading them in the Word of God and taking God at His word. This is the reason that it is so important to study the Scriptures. The Bible says that faith comes by hearing, and hearing by the Word of God.[7] The more we understand God and His Word, the more we have faith in Him—the more we trust Him.

Commands and Promises

Now let us consider some of the things that God has commanded us to do. We know that God loved the world so much that He gave His only begotten Son, that whoever believes in Him shall not perish but have everlasting life.[8] We know that He is not willing that any perish but that all should come to repentance.[9] We know that He has given us the command to go into all the world and preach the gospel and to make disciples of all the nations. He has promised to give us wisdom.[10] He has commanded us to be empowered and controlled by the Spirit as a way of life.[11] And He has promised that if we ask anything according to His will, He will hear us, and if He hears us, He has said that He will answer us.[12]

We can relate the commands of God to the promises of God and know that we are praying according to His will whenever what we ask contributes to a life of victory in Christ; a life that honors the Lord Jesus. True obedience will always lead to a fruitful life of introducing others to the Savior. In fact, anything that we do should contribute to the fulfillment of God's great purpose and plan for men and nations. Make a list of all the things that you believe God would have you do, as they relate to His commands. And then claim the promise of God that if we ask anything according to His will, He will hear and answer us. And begin to thank God for answering these prayers.

You do not need to beg God to answer your prayers. You do not need to plead with Him. He is far more ready to give than we are to receive. It is simply a matter of placing your confidence, your trust, in His trustworthiness—believing Him and praising Him, thanking Him in advance for His answers. Few of us ever even begin to comprehend what can be accomplished through prayer.

Top Priority

Prayer is without question the most important spiritual discipline in the life of a believer. This is said on the basis of the fact that our Savior Himself, though He is God, now seated at the right hand of the Father in the place of authority, is giving His time to intercessory prayer in behalf of all who believe.[13] Thus, if prayer is the highest priority in the life of our Lord, we should realize that the highest priority in the life of the Christian is believing prayer. I do not suggest that we need spend long hours each day in prayer, though some may be called to do this, and there is no higher calling—but all of us are commanded of God to pray without ceasing.[14] We are to bring everything to God in prayer. We are commanded to pray for one another.

"No amount of money, genius, or culture can move things for God. Holiness energizing the soul, the whole man aflame with love, with desire for more faith, more prayer, more zeal, more consecration—this is the secret of power. These we need and must have, and men must be the incarnation of this God-inflamed devotedness. God's advance has been stayed, His cause crippled, His name dishonored for their lack.

Genius (though the loftiest and most gifted), education (though the most learned and refined), position, dignity, place, honored names, cannot move this chariot of our God. It is a fiery one, and fiery forces only can move it. The genius of a Milton fails. The imperial strength of a Leo fails. Brainerd's spirit can move it. Brainerd's spirit was on fire for God, on fire for souls. Nothing earthly, worldly, selfish, came in to abate in the least the intensity of this all-impelling and all-consuming force and flame.

"Prayer is the creator as well as the channel for devotion. The spirit of devotion is the spirit of prayer. Prayer and devotion are united as soul and body are united, as life and heart are united. There is no real prayer without devotion, no devotion without prayer."[15]

It is said of Jonathan Goforth that once he felt assured of God's will in prayer, he would continue in the power of prayer until the thing was accomplished. Great things were accomplished through this man, for he was a man of powerful prayer.

George Mueller was an outstanding Christian leader in England, and was the head of a famous orphanage which cared for thousands of orphans. Mr. Mueller was a man given to prayer; and during his lifetime, he recorded over fifty thousand answers to prayer.[16] If your prayers are powerless, perhaps the difficulty is not in your prayers but in your life.

The following are qualities that contribute toward making a man powerful in prayer:

1. There must be no unconfessed sin in his life. The Bible says, "If I regard iniquity in my heart,

the Lord will not hear me."[17] Through the years different individuals have indicated to me that God has not heard their prayers. Always, as we have considered the reason, the answer has been quickly discovered: there is disobedience and unwillingness to confess sin in the life—unconfessed sin in the experience of the individual involved. If God is not answering your prayers, the first question you should ask yourself is, "Is there any sin in my life?" If there is, I John 1:9 assures us, "If we confess our sins, He [God] is faithful and just to forgive us our sins and to cleanse us from all unrighteousness."

2. He is controlled by the Spirit. We are told, "The Spirit itself maketh intercession for us with groanings which cannot be uttered."[18] We cannot know the mind of God and the will of God unless we are controlled by the Spirit.
3. He is a man of faith. We are told, "Without faith it is impossible to please Him: for he that cometh to God must believe that He is, and that He is a rewarder of them that diligently seek Him."[19] "And all things, whatsoever ye shall ask in prayer, believing, ye shall receive."[20] "According to your faith be it unto you."[21] The objective is not to be "great men of faith," but to be men who have faith in a great God!
4. He abides in Christ and lets His Word abide in him. Jesus said, "If ye abide in Me, and My words abide in you, ye shall ask what ye will, and it shall be done unto you."[22] Therefore, our lives must be yielded to Christ so that we will be in fellowship with Him at all times. As we medi-

tate upon His word with a thorough understanding of what He wants to accomplish in and through us and in the lives of men, we can ask what we will, and He promises to answer us.

5. Finally, he can be a man of power in prayer when he prays according to God's will as revealed in His Word. The Apostle John wrote, "And this is the confidence that we have in Him, that, if we ask anything according to His will, He heareth us: and if we know that He hear us, whatsoever we ask, we know that we have the petitions that we desired of Him."[23] Thus, it is important before we pray to determine the will of God and then in faith, according to the Word of God, expect God to answer. Faith lays hold of the promises of God with a thankful and expectant heart. The Scripture reminds us, "In *every* thing give thanks."[24]

Corporate Prayer

In Acts 12, we see a dramatic illustration of the power of corporate prayer. King Herod had ruled against some of the believers in Christ and had killed the Apostle James, who was John's brother. He had arrested Peter during the Passover celebration and imprisoned him, placing him under the guard of 16 soldiers. It was his intention to deliver Peter to the Jews for execution after the Passover. But earnest prayer was going up to God for Peter's safety all the time he was in prison. The night before he was to be executed, he was sleeping, double-chained between two soldiers, with others standing guard before the prison gate, when suddenly there was a light in the cell and an angel of the Lord stood beside Peter and said, "Quick, get up," and the chains fell off his wrists. Then the angel told him, "Get dressed and put on your shoes." And he did. "Now put on your coat and follow me," the angel ordered. So Peter left the cell and followed the angel, though all the time he thought it was a dream or a vision, and did not believe that it was really happening. They passed the first and second cell blocks and came to the iron gate to the street, and this opened to them of its own accord. So they passed through and walked along together for a block and then the angel left him. Peter finally realized what had happened. "It's really true," he said to himself. "The Lord has sent His angel and saved me from Herod and from what the Jews were hoping to do to me." After a little thought, he went to the home of Mary, mother of John and Mark, where many were gathered for a prayer meeting.

It was because of their united prayer that Peter was delivered. That same power of prayer is available to believers today, and many modern-day miracles have taken place in answer to prayer.

Power of Individual Prayer

You may wish to read of Moses' experience in prayer as recorded in Exodus 15:23-25. Here we find Moses leading the Israelites from the Dead Sea into the wilderness of Shur, and they came to the waters of Marah and found them to be bitter. And the people began to murmur against Moses saying, "What are we going to do?" Moses cried out to the Lord and asked

Him for wisdom and help. The Lord showed him a tree which, when he had cast it into the water, made the water sweet. God answered his prayers.

We are told that Elijah was a man subject to like passions such as we are, and he prayed earnestly that it might not rain. And it rained not on the earth by the space of three years and six months; and he prayed again, and the heavens gave rain, and the earth brought forth her fruit.[25] There was a spiritual lesson which God wanted to teach through Elijah and thus He answered this unusual prayer.

God Has No Limitation

You may have urgent personal problems or needs, or you may wish to release God's power to turn your campus or your community to Christ. You can know that you are praying according to the will of God if your heart is cleansed and you are controlled by the Spirit; if you are abiding in Christ and His Word is abiding in you; and if you are praying in faith, according to the Word of God. So make a list of the prayers you would like to have answered and begin to thank God when they are answered.

I remember well an experience I had many years ago when Campus Crusade for Christ was very small and our budget was modest. We needed $485. I was alone one morning in prayer, asking the Lord to send us this $485. At that precise moment, someone knocked at the door. There was a mailman with a registered letter from far off Zurich, Switzerland. A friend whom I had had the privilege of introducing to Christ had sent a $500 bank note, and it had just arrived, having originated some days earlier. It had arrived at the very time I was on my knees in prayer.

On another occasion the office manager had come to share an urgent and desperate need for $10,000. Through the years, we have never had any extra money in the ministry of Campus Crusade for Christ, even though our budget is now quite large with a staff of approximately 1,800 serving in 40 countries. We live from day to day, drawing upon the inexhaustible resources of God, preferring to trust Him rather than a large bank account or endowment. We believe that the Lord who called us to take the good news of Christ's love and forgiveness, who promised to go with us, who promised to meet our every need, is worthy of our trust. And so the office manager and I knelt together and said, "Father, we need $10,000; and You know where it is. Our desire is to please You and You alone, and we thank You in advance for sending this $10,000." About an hour later, as I was walking across the lobby of the Arrowhead Springs hotel, which is our International Headquarters, the telephone rang. A friend, thousands of miles away, said to me, "You have been on my heart and in my prayers for the last couple of days and it occurs to me that you may have a need. I felt impressed to call to ask you if there is anything I can do to help." I explained to him that my office manager and I had been in prayer less than an hour before, asking the Lord for the $10,000 which was needed immediately. "That is a lot of money," he said. "Let me see what I can do. I will call you back in an hour." An hour later he called to say that he would be sending a check for $10,000 the next morning in the form of a loan without interest and, should the Lord continue to bless his business interests, he hoped one day to be able to give it. A year later he cancelled the note.

Again and again through the years, hundreds of such experiences have demonstrated conclusively to me that God is omnipotent and that He has made available to us vast resources, and revolutionary power, to help change the world through prayer.

Prayer Promises Which You Will Want to Claim:

"If my people, which are called by My name, shall humble themselves, and pray, and seek My face, and turn from their wicked ways; then will I hear from heaven, and will forgive their sin, and will heal their land" (II Chronicles 7:14).

"Evening, and morning, and at noon, will I pray, and cry aloud: and He shall hear my voice" (Psalms 55:17).

"Then shall ye call upon Me, and ye shall go and pray unto Me, and I will hearken unto you" (Jeremiah 29:12).

"But thou, when thou prayest, enter into thy closet, and when thou hast shut thy door, pray to thy Father which is in secret; and thy Father which seeth in secret shall reward thee openly" (Matthew 6:6).

"Therefore I say unto you, What things soever ye desire, when ye pray, believe that ye receive them, and ye shall have them" (Mark 11:24).

"Likewise the Spirit also helpeth our infirmities: for we know not what we should pray for as we ought: but the Spirit itself maketh intercession for us with groanings which cannot be uttered" (Romans 8:26).

"The effectual fervent prayer of a righteous man availeth much" (James 4:16).

"If ye shall ask anything in My name I will do it" (John 14:14).

"If ye abide in Me, and My words abide in you, ye shall ask what ye will, and it shall be done unto you" (John 15:7).

"Hitherto have ye asked nothing in My name: ask, and ye shall receive, that your joy may be full (John 16:24).

"Again I say unto you, that if two of you shall agree on earth as touching anything that they shall ask, it shall be done for them of my Father which is in heaven" (Matthew 18:19).

[1] Jeremiah 33:3
[2] Matthew 28:19
[3] Matthew 28:18
[4] Matthew 28:20
[5] John 14:14
[6] Matthew 21:22, NAS
[7] Romans 10:17
[8] John 3:16
[9] II Peter 3:9
[10] James 1:5
[11] Ephesians 5:18
[12] I John 5:14,15
[13] Hebrews 7:25
[14] I Thessalonians 5:17
[15] E. M. Bounds: *Power Through Prayer*
[16] *Ten Basic Steps Toward Christian Maturity*
[17] Psalms 66:18
[18] Romans 8:26
[19] Hebrews 11:6
[20] Matthew 21:22
[21] Matthew 9:29
[22] John 15:7
[23] I John 5:14,15
[24] I Thessalonians 5:18
[25] James 5:17,18

Chapter 11

Revolutionary Outreach

There is nothing in this world more exciting than the adventure of sharing Christ with others. In many countries around the world I have asked two questions of tens of thousands of people: of old people and young, of rich and poor, of some of the most famous people in the world and of ordinary people like most of us. "What is the greatest experience of your life?" The answer of Christians has always been, "To know Christ—to know Christ as my Savior is absolutely the most important experience of my life." The second question, "What is the most important thing you can do to help another person?" The answer is always the same, "Help him to know Christ." Yet how sad it is that very few Christians are sharing Christ with others.

Every sincere believer in Christ knows that he should share his faith, but most do not. As a matter of fact, we are told that it takes over a thousand laymen and six pastors to introduce just one person to Christ in a year! Obviously there is something wrong.

If you are typical of the average Christian in the world, you have never introduced one person to Christ in your life. Yet, you would like to, for every true Christian knows in his heart that he should be introducing others to our Savior. Generally there are two good reasons why Christians are not fruitful in their witness: first, they are living defeated lives; and second, they do not know how to communicate their faith in Christ to others.

A Practical Formula

How can we experience an abundant life in Christ and share our faith more effectively with others? There is a spiritual formula which I would like to share with you. A formula which can change your life and your witness for Christ. Please do not misunderstand me. I am not trying to put God in a mold, because God is too big for our man-made molds. Yet, this is a scriptural formula that works. I can assure you that if you follow this scriptural formula, you will find that your life will be fruitful for God in a way that you have never yet experienced. What an adventure it is to introduce men and women to our Lord regularly, as a way of life.

I meet many people who are students of the Bible. They spend much time each day studying the Bible, yet they are not joyful. I meet people who spend time daily in protracted prayer who are not experiencing the abundant life. Yet, I have never met a person in my life who is sharing Christ regularly as a way of life, in the power and control of the Spirit, who is not radiant with joy.

One of my dear friends, who is one of the great Christian scholars of our day, said to a group of Christians gathered for training, "I am not fruitful in my witness for Christ nor am I experiencing joy in my Christian life." Later we talked about how he could communicate his faith more effectively with others and be more fruitful in his witness. For an hour or so we talked and considered various commands and promises of God's word. Then he went out on his own and shared his faith that afternoon with a couple of collegians. God touched his life. He came back that evening bubbling over with joy. He could hardly wait to tell us what God had done in his life. He shared how something wonderful had happened to him as he had talked to those young men about Christ.

Perhaps you spend hours in prayer or you may spend hours studying the Bible every day, but you say, "I am not joyful; I am not living that abundant life which Jesus promised and which you are talking about."

The formula I suggest, if followed carefully, will help you to become a joyful and fruitful Christian for as long as you live. But before I share this formula with you, I would like for you to consider with me a very appropriate passage found in Luke, the fifth chapter. Here we find our Savior speaking to a great multitude of people on the shore of Lake Gennesaret. This great crowd of people pressed in upon Him to hear the Word of God. He noticed two empty boats standing at the water's edge while the fishermen washed their nets. Stepping into one of the boats, Jesus requested Simon, its owner, to push out a little into the water, so that He could sit in the boat and speak to the crowds from there. When He had finished speaking, He said to Simon, "Now, go out where it is deeper and let down your nets and you will catch a lot of fish." "Sir," Simon replied, "we worked hard all last night and didn't catch a thing. But if You say so, we will try again." And this time, their nets were so full that they could not pull them into the boat. A shout for help brought their partners in the other boat, and soon both boats were filled with fish and on the verge of sinking. When Simon Peter realized what had happened, he fell on his knees before Jesus and said, "Oh, Sir, please leave us. I am too much of a sinner for You to be around." For he was awestruck with the size of their catch, as were the others with him. Jesus replied, "From now on you will be fishing for the souls of men." And as soon as they landed, they left everything and went with Him.

Some of you may be skeptical. For years you have fished for men but you have never introduced anyone to Christ. Now you hear me say that if you follow this formula you will be fruitful, and you are not prepared to believe that fishing for men can be so fruitful and so exciting.

Here is the formula for a fruitful life and witness:

First, be sure that you are a Christian.

Second, be sure that there is no sin in your life, unconfessed.

Third, be sure that you are filled with the Holy Spirit.

Fourth, be prepared to share your faith.

Fifth, make a prayer list of those whom you wish to introduce to Christ.

Sixth, go.

Seventh, talk about Jesus.
Eighth, expect God to use you.

Be Sure That You Are a Christian

There are millions of people who are active in the church but are not sure that they are Christians. I state this on the basis of years of interacting personally with thousands of professing Christians. In the course of the last year, we have had the privilege in institutes for evangelism all over the nation, and in several countries, to train some 75,000 laymen and pastors plus approximately 50,000 students. A good percentage of those, varying from five to ten percent, indicated in the course of the training program that they are not sure that they are Christians. Through the years it has been their practice, day after day, to pray "Lord, come into my life. I want to know You as my Savior." They hear a stirring sermon, they are moved by some experience of life, and they pray that prayer again, "Lord, come into my life." They are never sure that He hears their prayer and are thus never sure of their salvation.

John Wesley was one of the great servants of God, used perhaps more than any person since the Apostle Paul to reach men and nations for Christ. He was the son of a clergyman. His father and mother were saintly people. He was a member of the Holy Club of Oxford. It was his practice to fast and pray every Wednesday and Friday. He came to America as a missionary to the Indians, as he says in his autobiography, ". . . in the hope that I might save my own soul." But John Wesley did not become a Christian, according to his own words, until his life-changing experience at Aldersgate. There through the influence of Moravian missionaries, he read Martin Luther's treatise on faith as the introduction to the book of Romans, and his heart was strangely warmed. This man, who had tried to know God for years, met Christ and became a mighty servant of God to help change the whole course of history in England and many other countries of the world.

There are many people like this! I think, for example, of one of my dearest friends. During seminary days, we met often for prayer that God would do something very special for us--for our own spiritual needs, and also for the school. He was the son of a famous evangelist and came from a godly home. He had memorized thousands of verses of Scripture. He was one of those rare young men who lived such a disciplined life for God that he was a constant challenge and inspiration to me. He lived on multiple-purpose food for several days at a time, enabling him to live for twelve to fifteen cents a day. The balance of his allowance he gave to missions. He finished his theological studies for his B.D. and was studying for his doctorate in theology. One day he called me on the telephone and said, "Bill, I have just become a Christian." I replied, "Impossible, you are already one of the finest Christians whom I have ever known. You have had some kind of experience with the Person of the Holy Spirit." "No," he said, "I have just become a Christian." He went on to explain how all through the years, though he had never shared this, there was conflict, there was uncertainty, there was a lack of assurance that Christ was in his life.

A young woman came to join our staff. She was a most remarkable young woman. I remember when it was learned that she had made application, my wife and I commented, "What an outstanding person she is, and what a ministry she will have for God." She came from a wonderful Christian family, went to a Christian kindergarten, a Christian grade school, a Christian high school and Christian college. She had been active as one of the leaders of her church. She was the president of a Christian Women's group in her area. She was active as a counselor in some of the Billy Graham campaigns. She demonstrated most of those qualities that you would expect to find in a dynamic, radiant Christian.

I was speaking to the staff concerning the importance of giving assurance of salvation to those who are unsure, never taking for granted that those who profess to be Christians are Christians if they have any doubt about their salvation. I had told the staff not to try to convince them that they are Christians if they are not; but to help them to become Christians by taking them from their lack of assurance to full assurance of their salvation. This young woman came at the conclusion of my lecture with tears streaming down her cheeks, and she said, "I don't think that I am a Christian, and I have never been sure I was a Christian. From my youth, I have never been sure. I have gone to various pastors, and ministers of different churches which I have attended. I have gone to my father and other Christians and said, 'I'm not sure that I am a Christian.' And they would always say, 'You believe in Christ, don't you?' 'Yes.' 'Well, then, you are a Christian. Don't worry about it. Let's have prayer and you just believe that you are a Christian.' But it never worked." She continued, "I have become so distressed in recent months that I have been living on tranquilizers. I am afraid that I will die without God and I will be forever lost. I wouldn't dare take an airplane ride or do anything that would jeopardize or risk my life because I am afraid that I will die without Christ." I had the privilege of introducing this dear young woman who had been exposed to Christianity all her life, to the Christ of Christianity, and that night her heart was filled with joy and praise. She was so excited, she called her mother and father. She called my wife and others, to tell them what had happened.

There was a young man who came from Zurich, Switzerland, to the University of California for his doctorate in meteorology. He was a very gifted young man. He came to one of our retreats where he learned of Christ and received the Savior. Then he wrote his mother and father in Switzerland and told them what he had done. They wrote immediately in response to say they were coming to the United States to find Christ, too. Since he had mentioned my name in his letter as the one who had helped him, they asked if they could make an appointment with me. And so the son called to inquire if I would see his parents. He made it clear that they were not coming on a vacation or a business trip, but for the express purpose of meeting Christ. And so they came at the appointed time to my office. As we talked together, the father said to me, "I have been looking for God for years but I have not found Him. I went through a period of atheism which was not satisfactory, and in recent years my wife and I have been studying the various religions but we have found no answer. Some time ago we began to read the New Testament with considerable benefit. As a matter of fact," he said, "we concluded that Jesus had something to do with knowing God, and we said to our Bible teacher, 'We think Christ has something to do with our quest.' The Bible teacher said, 'I think perhaps you are right,' but we were not given any further help. And about that time the letter came from Hans. We have concluded that you are the one who can help us. Now," he said, "we have flown thousands of miles at great expense to hear what you have to say. We want you to tell us what you told Hans."

Well, you can imagine how I felt. What a privilege it was to talk to this wonderful couple, and later that evening, to their daughter, about our Savior—the living Christ. So I drew a circle, and in the circle I placed a throne, and on the throne, self—ego. And I explained to them that in order to become Christians they must be willing to surrender that throne to Christ. They must receive Him as their Savior. I explained that, according to the Scripture, ". . . as many as receive Him, to them gave He power to become the sons."[1] And Jesus said, "Behold, I stand at the door, and knock; if any man hear My voice, and open the door, I will come in to him, and will sup with him, and he with Me."[2] "Sir, you must invite Jesus into your life if you want to become a Christian," I explained. He replied, "Mr. Bright, I do that every day. As a matter of fact, I do it many times a day." Now I was puzzled. What could I possibly add to what he was already doing? They had flown thousands of miles from Zurich, Switzerland, to Los Angeles, They had spent a large sum of money to hear about Christ, and they were already doing what I had suggested they do.

Then suddenly, as I sat there praying even as I was talking to them, "Lord, You promised to give me wisdom, what do I say now?" there came into my mind this wonderful promise, "For by grace are ye saved through faith; and that not of yourselves: it is the gift of God; not of works, lest any man should boast."[3] Then I explained to them that it is not enough to invite Christ into your life. God honors faith. It is faith in the fact that He promised that if you would open the door He would come in that God honors. It is not the invitation. You can ask Jesus into your life a thousand times and He will never come unless you believe on the basis of His promise that He will come. He will not lie to you. I suggested to them that they invite Christ into their lives one more time and this time believe His promise, "If you open the door, I will come in," and ". . . to as many as receive Him, to them God gives the power to become His sons." I told them to place their trust in the promises of God and His faithfulness. The father sat back in his chair and laughed a holy laugh. He was filled with wonder and gratitude and relief and praise and thanksgiving. At last, he had found the One for whom he had sought all these years. Then he turned to his dear wife and spoke to her in German, for she did not understand English as well as he, and she responded in the same way. They met the Savior, and oh, how their lives were changed. Later that night I had the privilege of praying with their daughter who also received Christ. The entire family—father, mother, brother, sister—was united in Christ. Later I had the opportunity to visit them in Zurich and saw further the miracle of God's grace in their lives.

Becoming a Christian involves one's total personality —intellect, emotions and will.

It may well be that you have believed in Christ intellectually for years. You may be active in the church. You may be a moral, religious, godly person in the eyes of your neighbors, and yet you have never experienced this new birth. You have never been changed down inside. It is not enough to give intellectual assent to Christ's claims; nor even to have an emotional experience. There must be the commitment of the will before Christ will come. It can be compared to marriage.

Some years ago, I became aware of a young coed who is now my wife. I thought she was the most wonderful young woman in the world, and as I became better acquainted with her, I fell in love with her and she with me. But we were not married just because we admired each other or because we loved each other. It was not until one day we stood before a minister and exchanged vows—I said to her, "I do, until death do us part," and she said to me, "I do, until death do us part—" that in that moment, because of two words "I do," we became husband and wife. Two words changed the course of our lives. She left her home and I left my home and we started a third home. Now, there was no display of emotion when I said "I do." The walls didn't shake, the lightning didn't flash, there was no roar of thunder, I did not feel like jumping up and clicking my heels. As a matter of fact, I felt a little numb. But we were married, nonetheless. Those two words did it. She marched down the aisle on my arm, Mrs. William R. Bright. You know, I have not proposed to her since. I have told her that I love her, thousands of times. But one wedding ceremony was sufficient. My love for her has grown through the years since that moment when we said, "I do." So it is with Christ.

If you have never said to Christ, "I do receive You as my Savior," may I encourage you to do so right now. If you have asked Christ into your life scores or even hundreds of times, for the final—the very last—time, ask Him to come into your life, and then, on the authority of His promise, thank Him that He has come. He will not lie to you. Millions have received Him. Their lives have been changed as a result. After you have received Him, never ask Him into your life again. The rest of your life, you thank Him that He is there, for He promised never to leave you nor forsake you.

I was sharing this story in a city where scores of churches had united together for a city-wide institute for evangelism, and a woman who had reached the twilight years came to see me after my message. She told me that she had been a Sunday school teacher for more than forty years. Tears were coursing down her cheeks, as she said, "Do you know, seldom a day has passed in all these years that I have not asked Christ into my life?" She was so relieved that she never had to ask Him into her life again. That night she did ask Him in for the last time and she said, "The rest of my life, I am going to say, 'Thank You, Lord, that You are in my heart.'" Will you do the same? If you have never done it, do it now.

Accept God's Forgiveness and Cleansing by Faith

Second, be sure there is no sin in your life unconfessed. The Bible says, "If we confess our sins, He (God) is faithful and just to forgive us our sins, and to cleanse us from all unrighteousness."[4] As we read in Hebrews, Chapter 10, Christ came as God's sacrifice for our sins. In Old Testament times the Israelites took their sacrifice to the priest and the animal was slain and the blood was sprinkled on the altar as a covering for their sins. Christ came to this world to die as our sacrifice for sin. His blood was shed for our sins, and there is no need, since the cross, for additional sacrifices to be made for sins. There is absolutely nothing that I can do to add to what Christ did at the cross. My tears do not add anything; my self-imposed disciplines do not add to the cross. There is only one thing that I can do to make what Christ has accomplished for me a reality, and that is to confess my sins.

We know that the word "confess," in the original language, means to "agree with God." What do I do when I agree with God? *First,* I acknowledge that what I have done is wrong. When the Spirit of God says to me, with that still, small voice, "I am grieved with your conduct, your attitude," I can know that what I have done is wrong. God is holy. God does not look with favor upon sin. God loves the sinner, but He hates sin.

As we have already observed in the story of the prodigal son, even though this son had wasted his share of the inheritance in riotous living, when he returned home, the father embraced him and kissed him and held a banquet in his honor. This did not mean that he approved or condoned the wicked conduct of his son. Neither is God pleased with my sin. But He has made provision for it and when I agree with God, I acknowledge that sin is wrong, and that particular sin is grievous to the Lord. *Second,* I acknowledge that the sin which I have committed is paid for at the cross. And *third,* I thank Christ for dying for my sins. I turn from doing what I have done that has displeased God to doing what He wants me to do. I repent, and repentance means to turn around, to change my mind and my conduct. No man can be used of God who refuses to confess his sin, to turn from his sin.

There are those who say, "I don't have to confess because Christ has already forgiven me." It is true that Christ's death on the cross has provided forgiveness for our sins and there is nothing that we can do to add to what He has done. But that which is true from God's point of view as He looks at me through Christ becomes a reality in my experience only when I confess.

You show me a man who refuses to acknowledge his sin, who refuses to confess, who refuses to turn from that which grieves God, and I will show you a person who will soon be weighted down with guilt—who will soon be so frustrated and off course that God cannot use him. He will pray, and his prayers will not be answered. He may share his faith, but no one will respond. He cannot live a holy life and go on doing what he wants to do. Confession of sin is essential for a holy life and for a fruitful witness for God. The Scriptures say, "If I regard iniquity in my heart, the Lord will not hear me." The minute the Spirit of God puts His finger on your sin, confess it. Breathe spiritually. Exhale—confess your sins. Faith accepts God's promise that confession is followed by forgiveness and cleansing. Never confess the same sin more than once. Such a practice suggests unbelief which is displeasing to God. Faith pleases God.[6]

Be Filled with the Spirit

Though Jesus commanded the disciples to go into all the world and preach the gospel, He admonished them to wait in Jerusalem until they were endued with power from on high. His last words to the disciples were, "You shall receive power after the Holy Spirit is come upon you and you shall be My witnesses . . ." We cannot expect to be fruitful and effective for Christ unless we are controlled and empowered by the Holy Spirit.

Appropriate the fullness of God's Spirit by faith. It is as we breathe spiritually that we are enabled to know the power of God in our lives. It is as we continue to exhale by confession and inhale by appropriating the fullness of God's Spirit by faith that we can exercise the power that is available to us as children of God.

Be Prepared

By preparation I mean, learn how to present the gospel, the "good news," so simply that a child can understand. If you have not yet learned how to present the "Four Spiritual Laws," you can do so with a few minutes of instruction. Though I have shared Christ with others for almost 25 years, and have often spent hours sharing Christ with a single individual, I now use the "Four Laws" presentation almost exclusively. For many reasons the results are far greater.

One does not need to go to a theological seminary or to a Bible school to be used of God. I thank God for the way He is using some theological seminaries and Bible schools and other such Christian institutions, but you do not have to take long years of training before God can use you. Not everyone has the gift of evangelism. Not everyone is going to be a great evangelist. But all of us are commanded to be fruitful witnesses for Christ.

A few months ago, a young man stood up in a meeting in St. Andrew's Cathedral in Sydney, Australia, where we were conducting a large city-wide Lay Institute for Evangelism, and protested because I was insisting, according to the words of Jesus, that all of us are to be fruitful in our witness for Christ.[7] He said "Not everybody has the gift of evangelism," and I agreed with that. But I went on to explain that though all do not have the gift of evangelism, all of us are to be fruitful witnesses for Christ.

It is our responsibility as Christians to abide in Christ. It is our responsibility as Christians to follow Christ. It is our responsibility as Christians to allow Him to have control of our lives, to walk around in our bodies, to think with our minds, to love with our hearts, to speak with our lips. When we do this, He is the one who produces the fruit through us just as the vine produces fruit through the branches. Anyone can learn how to share his love for Christ with others, and it does not take a long period of time to do this. You can grow to maturity in Christ, and as you abide in Him you will always be prepared to witness.

Some Christians will be more fruitful than others. But do not be distressed if you find that some of your friends are introducing others to Christ more often than you do. Simply relax in the knowledge that those who come to Christ are the result of the Spirit of God working through you. You cannot boast and say, "Look at me, look what I am doing," when men come to Christ through your witness. Neither should you be defeated when you fail to see results each time you share the message. No, that is not your responsibility. It is your responsibility to follow Christ. It is His responsibility to bear fruit through you. He has no lips but ours. He has no feet but ours, no hands but ours. He has chosen to use man, and if we are obedient, He will use us. We can count on it. You will never experience failure when you witness, whether you see results or not, provided you share Christ in the power of the Holy Spirit. We are commanded to share Christ but the results are determined by the Holy Spirit. To put it more positively, we are always successful where we share Christ with others as we are controlled and empowered by the Holy Spirit.

Compile a Prayer List

The Bible tells us that God is not willing that any should perish, but that all should come to repentance.[8] If you want to be fruitful in your witness for Christ, make a prayer list. We have the promise that if we ask anything according to God's will, He hears us, and if He hears us, He answers us.[9] Do you want your loved ones, your neighbors, to come to Christ? Make a prayer list. Share Christ with them in the power of the Spirit. Begin to claim them for God. God will not deny Himself. You have the authority of His Word and His integrity behind His Word. You can share your faith in Christ with your loved ones and your friends, knowing that His promise is true.

I think of different loved ones for whom I have prayed, for whom I used to weep and with whom I have pleaded to come to Christ. They wanted to, but for some reason would not. Then the day came when I began to realize that God was not willing that they should perish. He loved them more than I, and so I began to thank God in faith that they will one day become Christians. That day has not yet come for some. It will, and I no longer weep. I now rejoice in the knowledge that one day they will come to Christ. God promised, and His word does not lie. One word of reminder. "If I regard iniquity in my heart, the Lord will not hear me."[10] Don't pray for the salvation of another until you have confessed any sins that the Holy Spirit has brought to your attention. Thank God for forgiving and cleansing you. Now, you are ready to pray.

Go to Them

If you want to be used of God, you must go to men. Do not wait for men to come to you. Go to them. One of the great barriers in witnessing is the problem of getting going. There are all kinds of excuses. We are all busy. Every man who wants to be used of God can be busy 24 hours a day on secondary matters and never get going to men. Christ commanded us to go. We need to rethink our priorities. We need to evaluate our investment of the 24 hours allotted to us each day.

How are we spending our time? Why not try dividing each day into 96, 15-minute periods for 7 days. Indicate what you do each 15-minute period and determine how much additional time you should invest taking the "good news" to men who are lost.,

There is a false teaching which suggests that you do not share your faith in Christ unless you receive some kind of revelation or emotional impression to witness to a person or group. Such a teaching is contrary to Scripture. Jesus said, "Follow Me, and I will make you to become fishers of men."[11] "Ye have not chosen Me but I have chosen you, and ordained you . . . to go . . ."[12] "You prove that you are My followers and bring great glory to God when you bear much fruit."[13] You need receive no further word from God than the Scriptures quoted above. Do not wait for an emotional leading, though such experiences may come to you as they have to me. Share your faith in Christ because you are grateful for what He has done for you and because you want to obey Him. This is my motivation and when I am alone with a person for more than a couple of minutes, I assume that God arranged our meeting in order that I might share Christ. Though I witness as a way of life daily, I seldom feel any impression to witness. Often my heart is cold and indifferent and I can think of a dozen good reasons why I should not talk to a particular person about Christ. However, soon after I begin to witness as an expression of my gratitude for what Christ has done for me and as an act of obedience to His command, I begin to sense His presence and power as He promised.[14] More often than not God graciously allows me to see fruit.

Talk about Christ

If you expect to reach men for Christ, you must talk about Christ. Do not talk about peripheral matters. There is a tendency to try to encourage others to become active in our churches. This is important, but this approach is not what reaches men for Christ. There are many people who are antagonistic to the church today, and if we are going to reach them for the Savior, we must talk about Christ, not the church. That will come, but in most cases, it will come after they have received Christ.

Do not talk about the Bible. You do not have to prove the Bible—just use it. Talk to men about the Savior. You will discover that not all people are ready to receive Christ the first time you talk to them. Not all of the fruit in an orchard is ripe the same day, neither are all of those with whom you share spiritually ripe. Some are ready to receive Christ, others are not.

As a young lad I used to visit my Uncle Ed's peach orchard. Every two days, we would go back to the same peach trees to pick ripe peaches. We would always pick the ripe ones, but we left the green ones. Two days later, we would go back to pick more ripe ones and two days later, additional ripe ones. So it is in our witness for Christ.

There are those who are ready to receive Christ now. Do not argue with those who are not ready. Do not badger them or insult them. Give them something to read, leave them with prayer, talk to them later—as the Lord gives opportunity—but keep on looking for the ripe ones. They are all around you, thousands of people are waiting to receive Christ.

No doubt the biggest and most devastating lie of the centuries is the lie of Satan that men do not want God. Most Christians have been conditioned to assume that others do not want to become Christians. The fact is, that most people want to know God. My eyes were opened to experience the hunger of men for God years ago when my wife and I started Campus Crusade for Christ at UCLA. As we began to speak to students in the various living groups, fraternities, sororities and dormitories, we discovered that approximately one half of the original group would remain after the initial presentation of the claims of Christ for a second meeting to receive Christ. That experience at UCLA has been duplicated on hundreds of campuses across America today and in over half of the major countries of the world where this ministry is now established. This hunger for God is not limited to collegians but exists at every age level—yes, many of your neighbors and loved ones are now ready to receive Christ. For example, recently a young soldier returning from Vietnam prayed to receive Christ on the plane and went on his way rejoicing. A few days later, I talked with a maid in my hotel room and she said she wanted to receive Christ. The following day a taxi driver and a young guide and his father prayed to receive Christ. Three different seat partners prayed to receive Christ on a plane flight from the west to the east coasts. Wherever I go, whether in planes or in buses, in hotel rooms, in lecture halls on the college campus, or among laymen, I find men waiting to receive Christ. This is true not only in my own personal experience; but members of our staff and those who receive our training, as well as countless others, are greatly used of God simply because they talk about Christ in the power of the Holy Spirit. They do not get involved with secondary issues. They know how to present the gospel clearly and simply. Talk about Christ in the power of the Spirit and the Holy Spirit promises to use you.

Some years ago I was invited to speak at a great university campus. When I arrived, there was a young man who was known as the campus atheist. He was a very brilliant philosophy student, older than most of the students, having been in the service. When he returned to the campus, he became the idol of the other students because he had a way of embarrassing their professors, and his fellow students seemed to like that. He would ask them questions they could not answer. I was asked to meet with this brilliant young skeptic to talk to him about Christ. As we met late one evening in the local campus coffee shop, he talked about philosophy, and I talked about Christ. When I stopped for breath, he would talk about his favorite philosopher or share his philosophy of life. When he stopped for breath, I would tell him about God's love and God's forgiveness in Christ. He gave no indication of interest in what I was saying. This rather unusual discussion continued for more than an hour. Finally I suggested that we call it a day. He asked if he could ride with us back to his dormitory, which was on the way to our destination. The director of our work had a two-door convertible; I got into the back seat. As this young man slipped in the front seat he turned around and said to me, "Mr. Bright, everything you said tonight hit me in the heart. I would like to become a Christian right now." We prayed together in the car and he received Christ.

I have seen many dramatic demonstrations of the power of God released when people talk about Jesus in the power of the Holy Spirit. Men who are antagonistic to God, saying they want nothing to do with religion, are dramatically changed as they receive Christ. A man in Australia said to me a few weeks ago, "I gave up all religion in World War II. I want nothing to do with a God that allows wars like this." I said, "Wait a minute; you are accusing God of something for which man is responsible." I began to share with him how I, too, had rejected religion, and I began to talk to him about the Person of Christ. His whole attitude changed, and he said he would like to pray a prayer and receive Christ as his Savior. Do not talk about peripheral things if you expect God to use you. Talk about the Savior—invite Him to express His love and concern through you.

Expect Results

Expect men to respond as you share Christ with them. A salesman would not be very effective if he approached a prospective customer with the question, "You don't want to buy any insurance today, do you?" Or, "You don't want to buy any brushes or any bananas today, do you?" Of course not. There are many Christians who go with that same attitude of unbelief. "You don't want to become a Christian, do you?"

Go with the knowledge that men are hungry for God. Men are receptive to the gospel if they are properly approached. They do not want religion, many of them do not want anything to do with the church at this point. They are not interested in the peripheral things, but men are interested in Jesus Christ, and if we bring them to grips with the Person of Christ, the majority are ready to respond.

It was said of our Savior that He could do no mighty things in Nazareth because of their unbelief. According to your faith, be it unto you. Do you expect God to use you? He will. Do you doubt that He will? He won't. Without faith it is impossible to please God. He that cometh to God must believe that He is, and that He is a rewarder of them that diligently seek Him.

If you want your life to be fruitful for our Savior:

Be sure that you are a Christian.

Be sure that you are filled with the Spirit.

Be sure that there is no sin in your life unconfessed.

Be prepared to share your faith in Christ.

Make a prayer list.

Go.

Talk about Christ.

Expect God to use you.

[1] John 1:12
[2] Revelation 3:20
[3] Ephesians 2:8,9
[4] I John 1:9
[5] Psalms 66:18
[6] Hebrews 11:6; Romans 14:23; Galatians 3:11
[7] Matthew 4:19; John 15:8
[8] II Peter 3:9
[9] I John 5:14, 15
[10] Psalms 66:18
[11] Matthew 4:19
[12] John 15:16
[13] John 15:8
[14] John 14:21

Chapter 12

Strategy for Revolution

We live today in the most revolutionary period of all the centuries. Revolution describes the mood of our times. World leaders are fearful of what tomorrow will bring. The late Sir Winston Churchill said, "Our generation may well live to see the end of what we now call civilization." There is fear that a madman will push a button, and the whole of mankind will be incinerated.

Former President Dwight D. Eisenhower said, "Without a moral and spiritual awakening, there is no hope of the world . . . one day we shall find ourselves disappearing in the dust of an atomic explosion." But, oh, what an hour for Christians to become involved in what could well become the greatest spiritual harvest since Pentecost. This is the hour for which Christians were born. Men's hearts are failing them for fear, and they are open to the gospel as seldom before in history. Now is the time for us to share the good news of God's love and forgiveness in Christ with even greater courage and boldness and faith.

Rome presented such a challenge in the first century. The command that was given to the disciples to go and preach the gospel, to make disciples of all nations, was used to turn a wicked Roman Empire upside down.

The Great Commission Given

Before His ascension, our Lord met with the disciples and gave them what we call the "Great Commission." Jesus said, "All authority . . . in heaven and earth has been given to Me. Go then and make disciples of all the nations, baptizing them into the name of the Father and of the Son and of the Holy Spirit; teaching them to observe everything that I have commanded you, and lo, I am with you all the days—perpetually, uniformly and on every occasion."[1]

Shortly after Jesus gave that command, the disciples began to preach this revolutionary message of God's love and forgiveness in Christ, and a spiritual revolution resulted. Rome trembled, tottered and fell; and the gospel of Christ triumphed.

God and the Holy Spirit took these men and women, who, before Pentecost, had denied our Lord and who, for the most part, deserted Him; and on the day of Pentecost, He caused something revolutionary to happen to them. They went out boldly to proclaim the gospel at the cost of their lives, and everyone of them died a martyr's death—except John who lived in exile. The result was a changed world.

The Great Commision Defined

At this point we should come to terms concerning

exactly what we mean by the Great Commission. For many years I have signed my letters, "Yours for fulfilling the Great Commission in this generation," and have frequently shared my conviction that we shall see the fulfillment of the Great Commission in our time. Considering the magnitude of the task with a population of approximately three billion, five hundred million people in 210 countries and protectorates, there are those who ridicule any such suggestion. I have been reminded that "the Great Commission has not been fulfilled since the first century and is not likely to be fulfilled in our generation either." As one good friend expressed it, "Bill, I thank God for your vision and applaud your efforts and the success of your ministry; but it is unrealistic to think that the gospel will be preached to every living person in this generation." With this statement I would agree, and it is because most Christians do not know what is involved in the fulfillment of the Great Commission, that we must first explain what we mean when we speak of the fulfillment of our Lord's command. Jesus gave the command to make disciples in all nations. How many disciples? Enough to saturate their entire community, city, state, or province and nation with the good news concerning Christ.

Will every person hear the gospel in our generation? No, there are people who because of physical or mental difficulties will not hear the gospel through human voices or written word. There are some individuals who live in remote and inaccessible areas of the world where they may not hear. Yet, when the majority of people in each country hear of Christ and many of these become disciples, the Great Commission will have been fulfilled. This does not mean that the majority will become Christians but that they will at least have had a chance to hear and to believe.

We must remember that Christ never expected us to Christianize all nations, but to evangelize them. As we faithfully proclaim the dynamic gospel of Jesus Christ to all men everywhere, not everyone will respond to its transforming message. Our responsibility is to preach and teach, and it is the responsibility of the Holy Spirit to make effective our witnessing. If we are consistent in our Christian life, faithful in our witnessing and dependent upon the wisdom and power of the Holy Spirit, we will not fail in fulfilling our part of the Great Commission. With the responsibility, Christ also gave all the equipment we need for success.

The Gospel Transforms

Christ changes men and nations; and wherever His message goes, men are changed. It was said of our Savior by the great missionary statesman, Dr. Samuel Zweimer, "The gospel not only converts the individual, but changes society. On every mission field from the days of William Carey, the missionaries have carried a real social gospel. They established standards of purity and hygiene, promoted industry, elevated womanhood, restrained antisocial customs, abolished cannibalism, human sacrifice and cruelty, organized famine relief, checked tribal wars, and changed the social structure of society."

Another historian, Phillip Schaff, author of *History of the Christian Church,* has said, "Jesus of Nazareth, without money and arms, conquered more millions than Alexander, Caesar, Mohammed and Napoleon. Without science and learning, He shed more light on things human and divine than all the philosophers and scholars combined. Without the eloquence of the schools, He spoke words of life such as were never spoken before nor since and produced effects which lie beyond the reach of orator or poet. Without writing a single line, He has set more pens in motion and furnished themes for more sermons, orations, discussions, works of art, learned volumes, and sweet songs of praise than the whole army of great men of ancient and modern time. Born in a manger, crucified as a malefactor, He now controls the destinies of the civilized world and rules a spiritual empire that embraces most of the inhabitants of the globe."

Most Christians have never taken the command of our Lord seriously. We have been playing at church while our world is aflame. A world that is threatening to disintegrate before our eyes is in need of the hope which only Christ can give and of a spiritual revolution which only He Himself is able to lead.

We are in the position today of men who are straightening pictures on the walls of a burning house. We are dealing with peripheral issues. It is the hearts of men that need to be changed. The problems of evil in the world that are threatening to engulf humanity can be solved only in Jesus Christ, and He has commanded His disciples to go and tell His message everywhere.

There are three good reasons why we must go. One, because Christ has given the command; two, because men are lost without Christ; and three, because men everywhere are hungry for God.

Christ Has Commanded

The athletic coach presents a list of standards, or requirements, to the athlete and says, "These are things you must do if you expect to make the team." The men subscribe to these rules, or they are not allowed to participate in the game. The employer says to the employee, "Here are the rules;" and the employee follows these rules if he expects to continue his employment. In time of battle, the commanding officer issues an order to the soldier, "This is what you shall do;" and he does it, or he is threatened with court-martial and may lose his life.

Christ has commanded Christians to "go," but most Christians have never heard Him with ears that hear.

No true believer in Christ can take lightly our Lord's command. From the time we awaken in the morning until we go to bed at night, if we take our Lord seriously, we have no alternative but to direct our attention, our time, our talent, our treasure, to the fulfillment of the Great Commission. We do this not out of a sense of legalism but out of a sense of gratitude and thanksgiving for what Christ has done for us and as an expression of our obedience to Him. He has said, "Go;" and that is enough. We need no other reason.

Men Are Lost without Christ

A young man said to Dwight L. Moody, who was counseling him concerning his need of Christ, "Mr.

Moody, do you think my father and mother really believe that I am lost? My father is the Sunday school superintendent of our church, and he has never talked to me about Christ. My mother teaches a Sunday school class, and she has never talked to me about Christ." He asked again, "Mr. Moody, do you really think that my mother and father believe that I am lost?" Has it ever occurred to you that some of your neighbors and loved ones who do not know Christ are lost according to the claims of our Savior?

Jesus said, "I am the way, the truth, and the life; no man cometh unto the Father but by Me." Now, that sounds narrow, doesn't it? But that is what Jesus said. For many years I have asked people all over the world if they have found God. Apart from those who have met Christ in a personal way, the answer is generally expressed in the following way, "I am looking for God, but I haven't found Him."

An experience which helps to further demonstrate that men are lost without Christ took place when I was speaking to a large group of students from several campuses in Southern California. On this occasion a young Muslim, along with many others, remained after the meeting to receive Christ. After all of the others had gone, he approached me saying, "I would like to talk with you in privacy." We went aside into a little room where we talked. He said, "I have come from a very devout Muslim family in my country. My father is a man of great influence and wealth; and I am here studying cinema, getting my master's degree. I have been looking for God for years, but I have never been able to find Him. Six months ago, when I came to the States, a doctor friend gave me a New Testament; and

I began to read it. As I read it, I became aware that Jesus is the God whom I am seeking. Tonight, as you spoke, it was as though He knocked at the door of my heart. I would like to ask Him in, but if I do, I must be prepared for many problems. I shall have to write my father and tell him what I have done, and he will disown me. If he disowns me, he will cut off my allowance. If I have no income, I will have to drop out of the university and will lose my coveted degree; and I will also lose my student visa and will have to go back to my country. In my country there are still devout Muslims who kill other Muslims when they become believers in Christ. If I receive Christ tonight, I must be prepared to give my life for my faith in Him."

Obviously, I did not press him; this was a matter far too serious for human intervention. I could only pray and ask God to continue and consummate His work in his heart. You see, God does not call you and me to "force" decisions for Christ. We are human instruments through whom the Holy Spirit does His work.

It seemed as though thirty minutes or so passed when, finally, the silence was broken by his words, "I am ready," he said. It was as though he were saying, having counted the cost, "I am ready to die, if need be, so that I might know Christ, so that I might know that my sins are forgiven, so that I might know that I have eternal life."

I must confess to you that we both wept as we knelt together in prayer. What an experience to realize that here was one for whom Christ was so important that he was willing to give his life, if need be, in order to know Him as His Savior.

Some time later, after he had endured much hardship and persecution, I asked him, "Are you sorry that you committed your life to Christ?" He assured me that He was not sorry. His father did disown him. He lost his financial support from his family; he was forced to leave the university; and he failed to complete his work for his long-sought degree in cinema. I regret to say that I lost contact with him. It is my understanding that he returned home to his country and very likely to his death. However, if he did die, he did not die in vain. My own commitment to Christ along with that of many others was made all the stronger. The word of God is emphatically clear. "There is salvation in no one else! Under all heaven there is no other name for men to call upon to save them."[2]

Men Are Hungry for God

Man's hunger for God has been demonstrated in thousands of ways since the beginning of the ministry of Campus Crusade for Christ. In the course of surveying tens of thousands of students on hundreds of campuses, we carefully tabulated 10,500 replies to 12 basic questions. Of those questioned, 89.5 percent said that they did not know how to become Christians, and more than 60 percent indicated that they were looking for a faith. The same great hunger exists in the lives of laymen across America.

As part of our training program at Arrowhead Springs and elsewhere, we spend several hours each week in actual person-to-person evangelism in local communities, at the beaches, and in public gatherings.

Hundreds often pray to receive Christ in a single afternoon. More than 1,000 people in the Watts area of Los Angeles prayed to receive Christ in a single afternoon through the personal contacts of 600 staff and students.

The average Christian has been conditioned to think negatively about the non-Christian's response to the gospel. This attitude prevails especially when seeking to reach students, intellectuals, and top executives. Yet, properly approached, the "leaders," whether on the campus or in the lay world, are usually the easiest to reach for Christ.

For example, I have seen more student body presidents reached for Christ for the amount of time invested than any other segment of the campus community.

Some time ago I was afforded a remarkable opportunity to see this demonstrated. The Vice President of the United States was slated to speak at a very important student convention to be attended by the top leadership of 133 colleges and universities. The student representatives from each campus were to include the student body president, editor of the newspaper, and a few other key students. A few weeks before the scheduled convention, the Vice President found it necessary to be released from this speaking assignment because of a very important White House assignment.

I received a call from the student body president at Stanford University, who was also the program chairman. Would I pinch-hit for the Vice President? Of course; I was honored to do so. But what would I say, on such short notice, to this select group of student leaders? I decided to speak to them of the greatest leader the world has ever known. My message on the

Person of Christ, who He is and why He came to this earth, lasted for forty-five minutes. When I finished there was a standing ovation, not, I am sure for the speaker but for the One about whom I spoke. Scores of these students stood in line for almost an hour to express their appreciation, and many of them expressed an interest in knowing Christ personally. Several prayed to receive Christ as a result. *Yes, men everywhere are hungry for God.*

In considering the Great Commission of our Lord, there are four basic truths that we should consider. There are four "alls." "*All* authority in heaven and earth is given to Me." "Go and make disciples in *all* the nations." "Teach them *all* things." And finally, "I will be with you *all* the days."

All Authority Belongs to Christ

Jesus said, "All authority in heaven and earth is given to Me." "I and My Father are One."[3] "He that hath seen Me hath seen the Father."[4] Seven times during the evening before His crucifixion, Jesus, in different words, promised, "If ye ask anything in My name, I will do it."[5]

The Apostle Paul writes to the church in Ephesus, "I pray that you will begin to understand how incredibly great His power is to help those who believe Him. It is that same mighty power that raised Christ from the dead and seated Him in the place of honor at God's right hand in heaven, far, far above any other king or ruler or dictator or leader. Yes, His honor is far more glorious than that of anyone else either in this world or in the world to come. And God has put all things under His feet and made Him the supreme Head of the church—which is His body, filled with Himself, the Author and Giver of everything everywhere."[6] To the Colossians, Paul wrote, "Christ is the exact likeness of the unseen God. . . . He existed before God made anything at all. And Christ Himself is the Creator who made everything in heaven and earth . . . in Him lie hidden all the mighty, untapped treasures of wisdom and knowledge . . . in Christ there is all of God in a human body; so you have everything when you have Christ, and you are filled with God through your union with Christ. He is the highest ruler over every other power."[7] When you go forth to represent the Lord Jesus Christ as His disciple, you can be assured that you are representing the One who possesses all power, wisdom, and authority. You have everything when you have Him. No power can resist you as you go in faith. Meditate on these and other similar passages. The more you understand who Christ is and all that He has done and will do for and through you, the more completely you will want to trust Him.

Make Disciples of All Nations

Jesus said, "Go . . . and teach all nations."[8] In order to make disciples, we must be disciples ourselves. Like begets like. We produce after our kind. The man who is committed to Christ, who understands how to walk in the fullness of the Spirit, is going to produce the same kind of Christian. Jesus said, "If any man will come after Me, let him deny himself, and take up his cross daily, and follow Me."[9] "Anyone who wants to be My follower must love Me far more than he does his own father, mother, wife, children, brothers, or sisters—yes, more than his own life—otherwise he cannot be My disciple."[10]

For some, such a call to discipleship may sound too hard. Perhaps this thought was in Peter's mind when he asked the Lord, "We left everything to follow You. What will we get out of it?" And Jesus replied, "Anyone who gives up his home, brothers, sisters, father, wife, children, or property to follow Me, shall receive a hundred times as much in return, and shall have eternal life."[11]

That this promise has been fulfilled in the lives of all who "seek first Christ and His kingdom," has been attested to times without number. Not always in material ways, of course, but in rewards far more meaningful and enriching.

I shall never forget the concern of the girl who later became my wife when I explained to her at the time of my proposal that I loved Jesus Christ more than I loved her and that He would always have first place in my life and in our home. Though she did not understand such a "fanatical" attitude on my part at that time, she later surrendered her life to Christ and now says with me, "Christ is first in my life." It is because of our individual commitment to and love for Him that we love and consider each other all the more. Truly Christ has enriched our individual lives and our ministry far beyond anything we could have dared to dream. We say with the famous missionary statesman, C. T. Studd, "If Christ be God and died for me, there is nothing too great that I can do for Him." The Great Commission will not be fulfilled until we become as interested in disciples as we are in decisions.

One hundred and eighty-five years ago, when William Carey began to pioneer the modern missionary movement, only 25 percent of the nations of the earth had heard the gospel of Christ. But today, every nation in the world, including Mongolia, has a testimony of Christ. Mongolia is receiving the gospel by way of radio from South Korea, by Mongolian refugees who were reached for Christ and are now preaching the gospel to their countrymen.

Even though there is a witness for Christ in every nation, the Great Commission is not fulfilled. We have only scratched the surface. There are thousands of villages, for example, in India where there is no word from God—they have never heard the name of Christ. In the great concrete jungles of Tokyo, Japan, there are more than 500,000 college students, the majority of whom do not know who Jesus Christ is. Multitudes of these Japanese, and people in every nation who are not yet Christians, will one day believe in Christ and become His disciples. The Great Commission remains unfulfilled until there are many disciples in every nation who evangelize their own countries through programs of total saturation with the gospel.

Teach All Things I Have Taught You

Then Jesus said, "Teach them to obey all the commands I have given you . . ." What are some of those commands? "Come unto Me, all ye that labor and are heavy laden and I will give you rest."[12] "Seek ye first the kingdom of God."[13] "Follow Me, and I will make you fishers of men."[14] "Love one another."[15] "Ask in My name."[16] "When ye pray, believe that ye receive

. . . and ye shall."[17] "He that abideth in Me, and I in him, the same bringeth forth much fruit."[18] "Herein is My Father glorified that ye bear much fruit; so shall ye be My disciples."[19] "Tarry ye in the city of Jerusalem, until ye be endued with power from on high . . . ye shall receive power, after that the Holy Ghost is come upon you; and ye shall be witnesses."[20] "Go ye therefore, and teach all nations."[21] These and many other important commands were given to the disciples, some of which are listed elsewhere in this book.

I Will Be with You All the Days

Finally, Jesus said, "I will be with you all the days." He did not say, "Go into all the world and good luck." He said, "I will go with you. I will never leave you. I will never forsake you." As a Christian, you are never alone. The forgiveness, power, and love of Christ are constantly available to you. No matter what you need, He is available to help you if you will only believe Him.

Our Strategy

Here is a strategy to help fulfill the Great Commission in our generation. In the United States, there are 3,000 campuses, representing over seven million students. These students represent the major source of manpower to help change the course of history. They need to be reached for Christ. It is the goal of Campus Crusade for Christ International to train key Christian leaders for each of these campuses; to organize evangelistic action groups; to take the gospel to every student through team meetings and personal contact, radio and films, correspondence and direct mail. Already hundreds of campuses and tens of thousands of students are hearing the gospel and responding.

Because of the phenomenal success of the student ministry, a lay ministry began in 1957. We began to hold one-day Lay Institutes for Evangelism and God began to bless in a remarkable way. The day-long Lay Institutes for Evangelism became weekend and week-long and, finally, city- and state-wide. Now God is working in the lives of thousands of laymen all over the nation. Our goal is to find highly qualified men to devote full time to this ministry, working with churches and other Christians in each of the 50 states and in each of the 224 metropolitan areas. These men are to devote their full energies and should be the most outstanding, the most dedicated men available. Further, our plans call for 177,000 volunteers for each of the political precincts in the nation so that there will be a trained worker qualified to train others to contact every person in every home, in every block, in every precinct, in every state, in the whole of the United States. Personal contact, correspondence, radio, television, films, direct mail, and every possible means of bringing the claims of Christ to men must be utilized. This entire strategy is designed to assist the local church.

The same basic strategy which we are using in the United States is planned for each of the 210 nations and protectorates of the entire world. Leading national Christians are being recruited and trained to direct this ministry in each country of the world. A ministry has already been established in more than half of the major countries of the world.

In addition to the student and lay ministry, we have developed a number of other ministries which are designed to accelerate the fulfillment of the Great Commission in this generation (see Appendix).

A Comprehensive Program

Through a multiplication program of *winning* men to Christ; *building* men in the faith; and *sending* them to the world with the "Good News" of God's love and forgiveness, tens of thousands have been introduced to our Lord Jesus Christ through the ministries of Campus Crusade for Christ.

Every conceivable program of *winning men to Christ* is used, including personal evangelism; large evangelistic meetings; evangelistic home Bible studies; action groups; films; radio; television; direct mail; evangelistic coffees, teas, breakfasts, luncheons, and banquets for both men and women; and literature distribution.

Building men in the Christian faith includes getting them involved in the fellowship and instruction offered through the local church, home Bible studies, and action groups. Christians are taught how to walk in the love of Christ and in the power of the Holy Spirit. They learn of God's unconditional love—His total forgiveness and acceptance made possible for us in Christ because of His death on the cross for our sins—and of His resurrection power available to us.

Christian growth is accelerated rapidly as individuals are instructed in how to share Christ with others and are encouraged to share their faith in Him regularly as a way of life.

Sending men to the world is the inevitable result of a proper emphasis on winning and building. The individual who rightly understands the love and forgiveness of God and who has been properly instructed in how to communicate his faith in Christ will not be satisfied with being a carnal, impotent, fruitless, mediocre Christian. Like the disciples whose nets were miraculously filled with fish, such an individual will "forsake all and follow Him."

Your Responsibility

Every sincere believer in Christ should be committed to the fulfillment of the Great Commission in this generation. The question to ask is, "Where can I begin?" Why not start where you live and share Christ with your loved ones, your neighbors and friends, and those with whom you work? Also, pray for the leaders of your community and the leaders of the world; and, wherever possible, share Christ with them. Each week, around the world, hundreds of outstanding students and successful business and professional people commit their lives to Jesus Christ through the unique ministry of Campus Crusade for Christ.

Campus Crusade for Christ staff believe that the Great Commission can be fulfilled in this generation. We have found that when the gospel is clearly and simply communicated, most men desire to know Christ personally. Without apology—boldly, yet tactfully—Campus Crusade for Christ staff present the Lord Jesus Christ as the only answer to life for time and eternity.

We invite you to join with us in helping to reach the

world for Christ. Thousands of additional staff members are urgently needed to fill exciting and creative assignments in ministries on campuses, at headquarters, and elsewhere around the world. With this ministry already established in more than half the major countries of the world, it is our prayerful plan to recruit 600 new staff members this year, and a total of 10,000 in 210 countries by 1976.

What in the world are you doing for Christ? Have you ever considered that God can use you to help change the world?

In this revolutionary, chaotic period of history, no sincere, thinking Christian dare be satisfied with the status quo, or business as usual.

Whoever you are, wherever you are, if you are available, God can use you—your time, your talents, your treasures—to help change this world. Changed men equal a changed society and a changed world. Only Jesus Christ can change men.

Your Personal Strategy

What about your own personal strategy for helping to fulfill the Great Commission? What do you plan to do? First of all, be sure that your life is fully surrendered to Christ. Be sure that you are filled with the Holy Spirit; then go to your pastor and offer your services. Make yourself available to your church. Make sharing your faith in Christ and the building of disciples a daily way of life. Begin to love by faith those with whom you work and play and live. Claim the power of God through faith to work miracles in your community. Begin to claim in prayer your loved ones, your neighbors, and your associates in business and professional life. Think beyond your city, your state, your nation to the world and believe God for the fulfillment of the Great Commission in this generation. Do not be satisfied with anything less.

We dare not be satisfied with business as usual. These are desperate times, and only our total surrender to Christ is adequate.

Some time ago, information regarding the phenomenal growth of communism was fed to the marvelous electronic brain, Univac, with the question, "What is the future of communism?" As you know, communism has expanded rapidly during the last fifty years. In 1903, Lenin started communism with 17 people. By 1917, he had taken over Russia with 40,000 followers. Today communists control over a third of the world's population, and most of the rest of the world has been influenced. Univac came back with the reply, "By 1970, communism will control two-thirds of the world's population. By 1973, its conquest of the world will be complete."

Today, communism has infiltrated every segment of society. The great student demonstrations and riots that are making headlines around the world are led, for the most part, by known communists in the United States and in most other countries. Three percent of the student population of China turned the tide and helped to capture one-fourth of the world's population—that great nation of China—for the communist cause. Think of it—three percent! In the United States alone, it is believed by many of the radical leaders that more than three percent of the students are already a part of the communist cause.

Why are they taking the world? Because of their dedication to the communist cause. For example, a young communist gives this answer. He broke his engagement with his fiancée, and the letter he wrote explaining his decision was given by her minister to Dr. Billy Graham. The communist student wrote: "We communists have a high casualty rate. We are the ones who get shot and hung and ridiculed and fired from our jobs and in every other way made as uncomfortable as possible. A certain percentage of us get killed or imprisoned. We live in virtual poverty. We turn back to the party every penny we make above what is absolutely necessary to keep us alive. We communists do not have the time or the money for many movies, or concerts, or T-bone steaks, or decent homes, or new cars. We have been described as fanatics. We are fanatics. Our lives are dominated by one great overshadowing factor: the struggle for world communism. We communists have a philosophy of life which no amount of money can buy. We have a cause to fight for, a definite purpose in life. We subordinate our petty personal selves into a great movement of humanity; and if our personal lives seem hard or our egos appear to suffer through subordination to the party, then we are adequately compensated by the thought that each of us in his small way is contributing to something new and true and better for mankind. There is one thing in which I am in dead earnest about, and that is the communist cause. It is my life, my business, my religion, my hobby, my sweetheart, my wife, and my mistress, my breath and meat. I work at it in the daytime and dream of it at night. Its hold on me grows, not lessens, as time goes on; therefore, I cannot carry on a friendship, a love affair, or even a conversation without relating it to this force which both drives and guides my life. I evaluate people, books, ideas, and actions according to how they affect the communist cause, and by their attitude toward it. I've already been in jail because of my ideals, and if necessary, I'm ready to go before a firing squad."

This is the reason the communists are taking the world; and let there be no mistake about it, they are out to take the world. However, most assuredly I do not believe that communism will ultimately triumph. Rather, I am absolutely convinced that the Great Commission will be fulfilled in our generation.

As one considers the phenomenal growth of communism and the moral and spiritual decadence that is threatening to destroy our civilization, one must be aware that we dare not play at church any longer. The only hope is an awakened church.

Dr. James Stewart of Scotland, one of the great New Testament scholars of our time, has said, "If we could but show the world that being committed to Christ is no tame, humdrum, sheltered monotony, but the most thrilling, exciting adventure the human spirit can ever know, those who have been standing outside the church and looking askance at Christ will come crowding in to pay allegiance; and we might well expect the greatest revival since Pentecost." I believe that. I believe that millions of Christians like ourselves are awakening to the fact that we must be about our Father's business. Like the Apostle Paul, we must tell others about Christ. He said, "Everywhere we go and to all who will listen we preach Christ; warning them and teaching them as well as we know how, so that we can present each one to God, perfect because of what Christ has done for each of them."[2]

Some time ago, I was visiting in Rome. One evening I sat in the Roman Forum; and there, through the medium of light and sound, I saw and heard portrayed the drama of ancient Rome. For almost a thousand years, Rome ruled the world. Into that Forum had come the conquering generals from their conquests to be honored and to receive their laurels. Into that Forum came the heads of various countries which made up the Empire. Here the senators met to legislate the laws that governed Rome. In that Forum, Julius Caesar had been assassinated. Here was a place that vibrated with history and drama. I was enthralled as I sat there. Earlier that afternoon, I had visited a dungeon cell across the road from the Forum, where it is believed that the Apostle Paul had spent the last few months of his life. Had I been living in those days, and had I visited Paul in the dungeon cell, it is not likely that I would have been as impressed with this "bond slave of Christ" as with many of the leaders of Rome. Paul was not eloquent of speech, according to his own admission; but here was a man with a brilliant mind, a flaming heart, and an anointed pen, a man who had linked his life up with the risen Christ. He was a man of God. He shared Christ's vision and burden for the world, and he was committed to the fulfillment of the Great Commission in obedience to Christ's command.

What God did in that dungeon cell had far more significance than did that which happened in the

Roman Forum. God took that life that was yielded to Him and used it to help change the course of history. Today we are Christians, worshiping Jesus Christ because, in some considerable measure, of what God did through the Apostle Paul.

Privilege of Discipleship

You and I have the privilege of being a part of the most significant movement of all the centuries, the movement to fulfill the Great Commission in this generation. I invite you to join with millions of other Christians in enlisting in the Great Commission Army. In behalf of our Lord and in His name, we are asking men everywhere to put aside their personal ambitions, their desires for their own pleasures, and to say with the Apostle Paul, "I want to be a slave of Jesus Christ. I will give my attention, my time, my treasure, my talents to Him for the fulfillment of the Great Commission. From the time I awaken in the morning until I go to bed at night, I want to be a part of this great strategy for the world."

Sacrifice and Martyrdom

It may mean sacrifice. For some, it may mean death —martyrdom—but can you think of anything more important? Can you think of a greater One whom you can follow? Is there a greater cause than His to which you can give yourself? If it is your desire to so commit yourself, may I suggest that you join with me in praying the following prayer:

"Dear Father in heaven, I stand at attention. I

make myself available to You to do with as You wish. I want to be a man (woman) of God through whom You can bring Your message of love and forgiveness in Christ to all men everywhere. I invite You to cleanse me, to empower me, to lead me, to inspire me, to teach me, to cause me to do that which will bring the greatest honor and glory to Your name. Enable me by Your Holy Spirit to contribute my maximum to the fulfillment of the Great Commission in my time. I ask this in the wonderful name of the Lord Jesus. Amen."

Great Commission Army

Do you, as an expression of your love and gratitude to Christ for what He has done for you and as an act of obedience to His command, want to help fulfill the Great Commission in this generation? If so, I want to help you. We are asking God to raise up an army of five million to volunteer for the Great Commission Army. We trust that they will represent each of the 177,000 precincts and will assist in sharing the good news of our Savior's love and forgiveness with the more than two hundred million Americans, and from our beloved land to the more than three billion five hundred million people in the other 209 countries and protectorates of the world. We would like to make our staff and training facilities available to help train you and other members of your church or Christian groups. We have nothing to promote and nothing to gain. Like the Apostle Paul, the love of Christ constrains us. We would like for you to come to Arrowhead Springs, our International Headquarters, for training in group and personal evangelism. Here you will learn:

1. How to live a Spirit-controlled and empowered life.
2. How to share your faith in Christ more effectively with others.
3. How to begin a witnessing experience.
4. How to present the claims of Christ clearly and simply.
5. How to avoid arguments and meaningless discussions.
6. How to help an interested person make a personal commitment to Christ.
7. How to help establish a new Christian in Christ.
8. How to build disciples.
9. How to plan a strategy for your personal ministry, church, community, city, state, nation, and world.
10. How to participate in door-to-door evangelism, telephone evangelism, Sunday school evangelism, evangelistic Bible studies, action groups, etc.

Remember, our world in revolution needs, and is ready for, the revolutionary message of our Savior's love and forgiveness. As one of His dedicated, committed revolutionaries, you can help change the world!

[1] Matthew 28:18–20, *Amplified Bible*
[2] Acts 4:12, *Living Gospels*
[3] John 10:30, *LNT*
[4] John 14:9
[5] John 14:14

[6] Ephesians 1:19-23, *LNT*
[7] Colossians 1:15,16; 2:3,9,10, *LNT*
[8] Matthew 9:23
[9] Luke 9:23
[10] Luke 14:26, *LNT*
[11] Matthew 19:27-29, *LNT*
[12] Matthew 11:28
[13] Matthew 6:33
[14] Matthew 4:19
[15] John 15:12
[16] John 16:26
[17] Mark 11:24
[18] John 15:5
[19] John 15:8
[20] Luke 24:49; Acts 1:8
[21] Matthew 28:19
[22] Colossians 1:28, *LNT*

Appendix

A Revolutionary Dream

The story of Campus Crusade for Christ International is a story which demonstrates the power, wisdom and grace of God. "For it is God who is at work within you, giving you the will and the power to achieve His purpose."[1]

This strategy—to help fulfill the Great Commission in this generation by winning, building, and sending students and laymen of the world for Christ—was not something fabricated by men, but was rather a commission of God, as has been demonstrated by His blessings on the ministry of Campus Crusade for Christ since its inception.

When a student in college, many honors came my way: editor of the college year book, student body president, "Who's Who in American Colleges and Universities," and others. I knew hundreds of students personally and counted many members of the faculty as special friends. Yet, I look back on my college career with much regret. Had I known the Lord Jesus Christ then, so much more of lasting and eternal significance could have been accomplished for Him during my college days.

Following my college graduation, I joined the faculty of Oklahoma State University, Extension Department. Later I pursued an active business career until, through my mother's prayers and the ministries of Dr. Henrietta C. Mears, Dr. Louis Evans, Sr., and others, the Lord Jesus Christ became my personal Savior. Immediately I was impressed to share this thrilling new life in Christ with others. For approximately five years, I was chairman of deputation work at the First Presbyterian Church of Hollywood where, with more than 100 other college students and adults, it was my regular practice to share Christ individually and with teams in other churches; as well as to "down and outers," on skid row, in the jails, and in road camps. Then one day I was awakened to the fact that, while thousands of Christians were giving their time to reaching these unfortunates for Christ, I knew only a few whose ministries were designed to reach the "up and outers," especially college students.

I remember well our first attempt to do something about reaching the students. We organized a special student deputation team which visited a number of the fraternity and sorority houses in the Los Angeles area. There we met with a gratifying response. However, in our inexperience, we did not know how to turn the interest of the students into commitments to Christ nor how to encourage them to grow in the Christian faith.

Various experiments to reach the students were

tried, and with each attempt we found ourselves closer to our objective of reaching the collegiate world for our Savior.

In the meantime, while continuing my business interests, I enrolled in Princeton Theological Seminary and later transferred to Fuller Theological Seminary in an effort to learn as much as possible about Christ and to prepare myself to serve Him as a layman. It was during my last year of seminary that something unusual happened in my life. There are certain sacred experiences of life which one is reluctant to share. However, this story would not be complete without at least a reference to that unforgettable experience with God in which Campus Crusade for Christ was born. Only one previous experience in my life could be compared with this. The other experience took place on a summer night, 1947, in Dr. Henrietta Mears' cabin at Forest Home. Present were Miss Mears, Louis Evans, Jr., Dick Halverson and myself. God met us in such a powerful way that night that all of our lives were revolutionized spiritually. Actually, a number of very significant developments in the Christian world have resulted directly and indirectly from what happened that night. So it was on this spring night, 1951, in our home in the Hollywood Hills. The hour was late. A seminary classmate and I were studying together for a Greek examination. Then, God spoke to me in a most illuminating way. It should be explained that God did not speak in audible words, but in a very real way He showed me that I was to devote my full time presenting Christ to collegians. Through developing the campus emphasis, the world could be reached for Christ. This was similar to my experience at Forest Home.

That night, the plan for reaching the collegiate world for Christ was given to me, and Campus Crusade for Christ International was born.

It is not easy to share such an experience, for there is always danger of being misunderstood. Further, there is always the chance that other Christians may seek such an experience for themselves. To do so would be most unwise, for the Christian is to live by faith, and the very act of seeking an experience denies the principle of faith. However, it is only for the glory of God that this is being told. For several weeks I prayed for guidance and met daily with seminary classmates, Dan Fuller, Hugh Brom and Bill Savage, to pray concerning this commission of God to reach the universities of the world with the gospel. Though lacking only a few units for graduation, I felt compelled to leave seminary to launch the ministry of Campus Crusade for Christ.

Dr. Wilbur Smith, Dr. Henrietta C. Mears, Dr. Billy Graham, Dr. Dick Halverson, Dawson Trotman, Cy Nelson, Dan Fuller, Dr. Edwin Orr and a number of other outstanding Christian leaders agreed to serve on the advisory board of Campus Crusade for Christ. Since that beginning, a number of additional leaders in the Christian world have joined forces with us.

In an unusual way, the Lord made available a lovely home near the UCLA campus as a base of operation for the work. We began immediately by starting a 24-hour chain of prayer and by organizing four teams to visit the various groups living on the campus. The response was overwhelming; scores of students expressed their desire to become Christians. Among them were top athletes, the student body president, editor of the newspaper and a number of other campus leaders. By the end of the year, no one doubted that God had visited UCLA in a mighty way, as over 250 students had made decisions for Christ.

Campus Crusade for Christ is an aggressively evangelistic movement, which places a strong, wholesome emphasis on the living Christ, the authority of the Scriptures, the importance of the church, personal and group evangelism, the ministry of the Holy Spirit and the adventure of Christian discipleship. Campus Crusade is an evangelistic arm of the church, which, because of the interdenominational nature of its emphasis, is able to reach large segments of the nonchurched student and lay worlds which normally would not be receptive to similar approaches from denominational groups.

The message of Christ is presented to the world through every possible means, utilizing every modern medium of communication. Beginning with the college campus, Campus Crusade for Christ has expanded to include manifold ministries which enter every avenue of interest and approach.

Campus Ministry

The college campus is the scene of revolution today —both for good and for evil. All around the world, the forces of materialism, secularism, atheism, and communism are battling for the minds of students. Campus Crusade for Christ concentrates on reaching these key future leaders for Christ because:

1. Students are the best source of manpower to help fulfill the Great Commission.
2. Apart from children, students are the most receptive to the gospel.
3. Students are unencumbered—free to invest their lives for Christ.
4. Students are receptive to truth and are mature enough to make wise decisions.
5. Today's students are assuredly tomorrow's leaders in every field.
6. Students—while they are still students—have increasing influence.
7. Students from many cities and foreign lands are concentrated in large groups on the campus.

Campus Crusade for Christ staff members are serving on strategic campuses all across the nation and in more than half of the major countries of the world. It is their privilege daily to introduce students to Jesus Christ.

Staff members talk to tens of thousands of students and professors each year in person-to-person interviews and living group situations. Thousands of those who receive Christ, including many activists and leaders in government, athletics, communications, etc., become disciples through a carefully planned follow-up program. They, in turn, win and disciple others. The result: spiritual multiplication and spiritual revolution.

All over the country, many thousands of young men and women have spent years developing and perfecting athletic skills. The ministry of Campus Crusade for

Christ provides opportunities for these skills to be used to help change the world!

Campus Crusade's American Athletes in Action basketball and wrestling teams tour the country each season competing against major college and university teams and compiling very good records. At every contest these athletes share the gospel of Jesus Christ with spectators. They have spoken of His love to millions in person, and on radio and TV. More teams in more sports are planned as other athletes join the staff.

Coaches, journalists, secretaries, and people with many other skills and abilities take part in planning and developing this sports program as well as in following through on those who are introduced to Jesus Christ. Others are participating in the development of a junior athletic program for young teenagers. Special campus representatives work with athletic groups at colleges and universities all over the United States.

Audio-Visual Ministry

All around the world, people are responding to messages presented through the media of films and tapes. Our Audio-Visual ministry continually seeks new concepts and methods of utilizing these and other media to help introduce people to Jesus Christ and to teach them how they can experience and share the abundant life which He offers.

We are constantly exploring the possibilities of all modern electronic methods of communication for reaching the world. Creative people, trained in all phases of development and production in these media, are finding their abilities and productive talents stretched by the opportunities and challenges here at Arrowhead Springs. As each new person joins the Audio-Visual staff, he finds opportunities for utilization of the skills and abilities which God has given him. We are convinced that effective utilization of these media of communication is essential to fulfilling the Great Commission in this generation—and that Christians who are effective in this field can find no better place of service!

Faculty Staff

The Faculty Staff, both associate (remaining in faculty positions) and full-time, are participating directly in the campus outreach, taking an aggressive role in introducing professors and students to Christ. Our present goal is a full-time faculty staff member on every district team and at least one associate staff member on every campus!

Crusade Training Group

The Crusade Training Group provides a unique opportunity for a positive work and training experience for young adults who, for some reason, find themselves uncertain as to God's ultimate place of service for them, with uncommitted time, or in a period of transition.

Participants in this program fill vital needs at the International Headquarters, carrying a regular work load. In addition, they receive valuable encouragement in their spiritual development through Bible studies, action groups, Institute of Biblical Studies courses, church activities, and participation in the regular programs for the staff at headquarters.

Members of the Crusade Training Group should have a teachable attitude and a desire to be used of God. They receive room and board and a small salary and agree to remain at Arrowhead Springs for a minimum of three months.

High School Ministry

The High School Ministry of Campus Crusade for Christ seeks to evangelize the high school youth of America. It cooperates with the churches, is locally advised, student-promoted, staff-led, and is often inspired by the help of college students. There are presently two forms of ministry: (1) organizing, training, and leading youth in citywide youth crusades; (2) working with local churches and communities in forming a youth program that is school-oriented and aimed at carrying on a continuous program of evangelism. Staff members and teenagers share Christ with their friends and seek to establish them into the fellowship of the church for further follow-up.

Implementation of these programs requires staff members with a wide variety of skills and abilities. High School Ministry representatives learn how to relate to non-Christian and disinterested high school students so that the gospel can be communicated. Follow-up programs require intensive individual contact with new Christians in order to help them to grow and to teach them how to introduce others to Christ. Teenagers are taught to speak with their friends about Christ and to share their faith. Small action groups are organized, and staff members participate directly, becoming close friends with teenagers, helping them with the day-to-day problems of life.

International Headquarters

In headquarters offices, secretaries, office managers, and others are finding their skills used directly in helping to fulfill the Great Commission in this generation. They are finding their ingenuity and ability stretched by new challenges every day. These men and women actively participate in the initiation and development of expanded programs of evangelism and follow-up.

Publications, including a newspaper and three action-oriented magazines, require journalists, graphic artists, editors, and others associated with the production and distribution of printed materials.

Electricians, plumbers, gardeners, carpenters, and other skilled craftsmen utilize their talents to help operate the International Headquarters. Some have left budding careers as the Lord has called them to this movement. Others have come here upon retirement, bringing a lifetime of knowledge and skill development to this new ministry. Many more positions in these fields will open this year as God expands our opportunities around the world.

Computer applications offer opportunities for programmers, operators, and other skilled people to use their talents and abilities in this world-changing movement.

International Ministry Overseas

The vision and ministry of Campus Crusade for Christ is international in scope. Our objective is to recruit and train key nationals in every country who will in turn recruit and train others to take the message of Jesus Christ to the students and laymen in their respective nations. Currently, Campus Crusade for Christ, under national leadership, is reaching students in more than half of the major countries of the world. As staff members become available, we are trusting God to establish this ministry in all of the 210 countries and protectorates of the world.

In addition, experienced American staff members have opportunities to assist national staff in other countries. Secretarial help is also urgently needed at International Headquarters.

In the United States

The mission fields of the world have come to the campuses of America. Approximately 115,000 students from almost every country in the world are studying in our colleges and universities. Most of these will return to their own countries to assume positions of leadership in government, business, and various professions.

These students can be reached for Christ now, while they are in the United States, more readily than in their own countries. Write today—volunteer your help to introduce internationals to Christ on your campus and in your home.

Lay Ministry

As a major part of our role in serving the church of

Jesus Christ, Campus Crusade for Christ has developed an effective worldwide ministry among laymen and pastors, helping them to become part of a spiritual revolution. Special attention is given to the importance of the church. The Lay Institutes for Evangelism teach laymen how to help others to:

a. Know Jesus Christ personally as Lord and Savior.
b. Live in the power of the Holy Spirit.
c. Introduce others to Jesus Christ.
d. Love by faith.
e. Be part of a strategy to help fulfill the Great Commission in our time.
f. Engage in "spiritual multiplication."

Military Ministry

All around the world, members of our Military Ministry are sharing Christ with men who live in the shadow of death.

Basic strategy at present is fourfold: (1) sharing Christ with servicemen on bases at the invitation of chaplains; (2) training officers and enlisted men in personal evangelism through seminars and institutes; (3) conducting evangelistic meetings on installations through teams of Christian military men; and (4) reaching military wives and dependents through a musical program called "Fantasia in Red, White and Blue."

Retired military personnel and men who have completed their obligated active military service have had outstanding success as members of our military staff.

Many men and women now serving in the military are also associate staff with Campus Crusade for Christ and are finding that God uses them in unusual ways to introduce other service people to Christ. Men and women of outstanding musical and dramatic talent are finding places in the Fantasia ministry. Personnel in the headquarters office are discovering that abilities of all kinds can be useful in coordinating activities to reach military men around the world.

Radio And TV Ministry

"Challenge for Today," our weekly fifteen-minute broadcast, is now heard on approximately 200 radio stations across America. Each broadcast includes a message from Bill Bright; personal comments from laymen, pastors, and students; special reports telephoned from campuses in the United States; and the tapes from foreign countries.

Growth in this program and the initiation of a new evangelistic sports program requires more qualified personnel in the radio ministry. As God leads qualified people to join the staff, they become involved in creating effective programming to help give the gospel a hearing among people who would not otherwise hear.

Now a nationwide one-hour television program has been videotaped, entitled "Campus Crusade: a New Kind of Revolution." This originated directly from the UCLA campus, and other projected programs will originate from campuses all around the United States. We trust that many able people from all phases of television production will be led by God to become part of the team to produce this series.

Musical Ministry

The New Folk and The Forerunners singing groups for Campus Crusade for Christ have an exciting ministry as they perform and speak before audiences in every part of the United States and throughout Europe. Participants in this ministry uniquely express the gospel through folk and popular songs arranged especially for this purpose.

In addition to these performances, members of the groups spend time in direct campus outreach, speaking to individual students.

As the number of outstandingly talented applicants increases, the number and diversity of touring groups also increase. An even wider variety of musical ministries is planned for the future.

The Importance of the Church

Campus Crusade for Christ places a strong emphasis on the importance of the church. As a matter of policy, each staff member is required to be actively involved in an established local church and to use his influence to encourage new and older Christians to follow the same practice.

The Blessing of God

The question is often asked, "What are the results of the Campus Crusade for Christ ministry?" Beginning at UCLA in 1951, the Crusade ministry has spread to hundreds of leading campuses across the nation, and into more than half the major countries of the world. Tens of thousands of students and laymen have heard the claims of Christ through representatives of Campus Crusade for Christ. Many thousands are now experiencing the full and abundant life which Christ alone can give. Hundreds of these are presently engaged in sharing Christ in various types of Christian service. Others are continuing their Christian training in order to increase their effectiveness for Christ. Thousands who have become Christians through the Crusade ministries can be found making a vital witness for Christ in the business and professional world.

The Future

Our vision for helping to evangelize the world for Christ in this generation is clear. We face a world desperately in need of Jesus Christ. We live in a period of history unique for its challenges and opportunities. We have a great, omnipotent God and loving Heavenly Father who is willing that none should perish. We have a dynamic gospel to proclaim—a message that is the power of God unto salvation.

Let us join hands and hearts, in the power of the Holy Spirit and in the love of Christ, to help change the world. Let us believe God for *Spiritual Revolution Now.*

[1] Philippians 2:13, *Phillips*

AS A RESULT OF READING **REVOLUTION NOW!**

- ☐ I have received Jesus Christ as my Savior.
- ☐ I have appropriated the fullness of the Holy Spirit into my life.
- ☐ I want to be a part of helping to fulfill the Great Commission in my generation.
- ☐ Please send additional information and material to assist me in my Christian growth.

Name . . . .

Address . . . .

City . . . . State . . . . Zip . . . . .

Telephone . . . . Age Group: ☐ Youth ☐ High School ☐ College ☐ Adult

FIRST CLASS
Permit No. 1031
San Bernardino
Calif. 92404

BUSINESS REPLY CARD

No Postage Stamp Necessary if Mailed in the United States

POSTAGE WILL BE PAID BY—

CAMPUS CRUSADE FOR CHRIST INTERNATIONAL

Arrowhead Springs

San Bernardino, California 92404